The Case of the
Chocolate Cream Killer

For Mum & Lexi

The Case of the Chocolate Cream Killer

The Poisonous Passion of Christiana Edmunds

Kaye Jones

PEN & SWORD
HISTORY

First published in Great Britain in 2016 by
Pen & Sword History
an imprint of
Pen & Sword Books Ltd
47 Church Street
Barnsley
South Yorkshire
S70 2AS

Copyright © Kaye Jones 2016

ISBN 978 1 78159 375 2

Typeset in Ehrhardt by
Mac Style Ltd, Bridlington, East Yorkshire
Printed and bound in the UK by CPI Group (UK) Ltd,
Croydon, CRO 4YY

Pen & Sword Books Ltd incorporates the imprints of Pen & Sword
Archaeology, Atlas, Aviation, Battleground, Discovery, Family
History, History, Maritime, Military, Naval, Politics, Railways,
Select, Transport, True Crime, and Fiction, Frontline Books, Leo
Cooper, Praetorian Press, Seaforth Publishing and Wharncliffe.

For a complete list of Pen & Sword titles please contact
PEN & SWORD BOOKS LIMITED
47 Church Street, Barnsley, South Yorkshire, S70 2AS, England
E-mail: enquiries@pen-and-sword.co.uk
Website: www.pen-and-sword.co.uk

Contents

Acknowledgements   vi

15 March 1847   vii

Chapter 1   "An Easy and Indifferent Childhood"   1

Chapter 2   "Where Insanity Has Prevailed"   12

Chapter 3   "A Creature of Leisure"   25

Chapter 4   "Exciting the Passions"   37

Chapter 5   "A Scattering of Death"   49

Chapter 6   "For the Pure Love of Deception"   59

Chapter 7   "Who Knows Where This May End"   72

Chapter 8   "A Delicate Thing to Allude to"   82

Chapter 9   "Most Extraordinary and Most Serious Charges"   92

Chapter 10 "The Border Land Between Crime and Insanity"   106

Chapter 11 "A Grievous Tale to Tell"   120

Chapter 12 "The Venus of Broadmoor"   132

Epilogue   143
Notes   146
Bibliography   155
Index   160

Acknowledgements

I have spent the last two years writing Christiana's story and there are a number of people that I would like to thank for all their help and support during this time. Firstly, to Pen & Sword Books, who gave me this fantastic opportunity, and to my lovely editors, Jen Newby and Eloise Hansen, for all of their help, advice and encouragement along the way.

Researching Christiana's life, especially her early years in Kent, proved very tricky and I thank Anthony Lee, of Margate Local History, for sharing his excellent knowledge on her father and allowing me to use many of his photographs. To Luke Mouland, of Kith and Kin Research, I bow to your genealogical superiority and thank you for all your assistance. I also thank Alannah Tomkins for allowing me access to her research on the sad fate of Dr Charles Beard and to Mark Stevens for pointing me in the right direction. My thanks also to Peter Henderson of the King's School Archives for information on the young William Edmunds. I also appreciate the efforts of staff at the Kent Archives, The Keep in Brighton and the Berkshire Record Office, who supplied me with so much information.

Finally, to my (long-suffering) family and friends, especially Keiran, Lexi, Liz, and Janine; I will never be able to fully express my gratitude for all of your patience and support while writing this book. I could not have done it (and stayed sane) without you all and I promise no more stories of syphilis and strychnine. Not until the next book, anyway.

15 March 1847

The death of a patient was not an unusual occurrence at Peckham House Lunatic Asylum.

Inside the walls of this former private mansion, the asylum's resident physician, Dr James Hill, was occupied with the macabre task of certifying a death, a task he had carried out more times than he cared to remember. The patient who had tonight lost his life was William Edmunds and the doctor felt a pang of genuine sadness as he stood over his lifeless body. It was not that Dr Hill favoured William above his other patients; he prided himself upon the equal treatment of all those in his care. It was, in fact, the cause and manner of William's passing that had provoked such an emotional response in the usually calm and reserved doctor.

Since his arrival at Peckham House six years earlier, Dr Hill had seen scores of men afflicted by the same tragic ailment as William. Its medical name was general paralysis of the insane, though those who had witnessed first-hand its devastating impact knew it as "one of the most terrible maladies that can afflict a human being".[1] General paralysis of the insane was first recognised in 1672 by the physician, Thomas Willis, but was not studied again until 1798 when John Haslam, an apothecary to the infamous Bethlem Hospital, described three cases in his book *Observations on Insanity*. After Haslam, it was the French who took the lead: beginning in 1822 with Antoine Bayle, a physician working in Paris, who recognised general paralysis as a distinct disease and offered the first clinical description of its symptoms.[2] It was these symptoms which fascinated doctors on both sides of the Channel.

They were bizarre, yet debilitating, and almost always resulted in the premature death of the patient. By the early nineteenth century, then, the peculiar course of this disease was well-understood and had been well-documented by physicians in England and France.[3]

It all began with paralysis of the tongue. Unable to move this major muscle, the patient would start to stammer and mutter like a 'person intoxicated'.[4] Accompanying this strange paralysis were delusions of grandeur which caused the patient to rave and boast of vast, though imagined, wealth and riches. As these symptoms developed, a second stage of the disease set in. The paralysis spread to the upper and lower limbs and weakened the muscles of the neck and trunk. This made basic physical movements, like sitting upright and standing, extremely difficult. Mental deterioration also continued, with most patients now in the advanced stages of dementia and in need of constant care. 'Nothing is more deplorable than the aspect of a lunatic affected with general paralysis of the third degree', wrote the eminent physician, James Cowles Prichard, in 1835. His observations demonstrated the full horror of the disease's final stage:

> *These patients, motionless and insensible, are reduced to a state of mere vegetation; their existence is a kind of slow death … Some individuals are not able to utter a single word, and only utter vague and confused sounds. The lower extremities are so weak that standing is impossible … Often there remains no trace of intelligence.*[5]

Physicians and asylum attendants could offer only palliative care to patients in this final and most disabling stage of general paralysis. There was no hope of a cure and no way of knowing how long they might survive. From the onset of first symptoms, life expectancy ranged from eight months to three years, though a minority had survived a year or two longer.[6] With such ferocity then, it is hardly surprising that general paralysis became a great source of concern for medical professionals who estimated that it accounted for 20 per cent of asylum admissions.[7] The constant care required by patients, particularly in the latter stages, placed a great burden on asylum resources and gave the worrying impression that these institutions were teeming with incurable cases.[8] Although the number of general paralysis diagnoses did increase in the mid-nineteenth century, so too did the general level of insanity among the population. In 1800, for example, there were 2 to 3 people per 10,000 diagnosed as insane in England and Wales. By 1845, this figure had increased to 13 per 10,000 and, by the end of the century, had more than doubled to 30.[9] In the minds of England's physicians and asylum superintendents, however, the rapid progression and bleak prognosis of general paralysis made it a far worse adversary than other disorders of the mind.

At 47 years old, William Edmunds fit the typical profile of a general paralysis patient. From the earliest observations on the wards of Parisian asylums, it was clear that this disease preyed almost exclusively on men in middle age. This deeply concerned medical professionals who saw countless husbands and fathers in the prime of life cruelly snatched away from their families. Dr Hill at Peckham House, felt content in the knowledge that his patient's suffering was now over – but there would be one final twist in the tale of William Edmunds. In 1857, ten years after his death, in 1857, the cause of general paralysis of the insane would finally be revealed when two German surgeons, Johann Esmarch and Willers Jessen, established a causal link between general paralysis and syphilis, one of the most contagious and prevalent infections of the nineteenth century.[10] Long after William's demise, the implications of this revelation would come to define the Edmunds family and expose a legacy of lunacy, tragedy and murder.

Chapter One

"An Easy and Indifferent Childhood"

The pretty, seaside town of Margate was less than eighty miles from Peckham House and it was the place that William Edmunds had once called home. Over the previous century, Margate had undergone a rapid transformation and, by the time of William's birth in 1801, had emerged as one of England's most popular seaside locations. It was the revival of sea-bathing in the 1730s that had prompted this dramatic change of fortunes, bringing an army of day-trippers and holiday-makers to the town, eager to reap the curative benefits of its clean, blue sea and sandy shore.

The town's increasing popularity and prominence provided new opportunities for Margate's native families too. William's father, Thomas Edmunds, was a well-respected and successful carpenter who had profited from the town's building boom in the late-eighteenth century. The Edmunds family home in Hawley Square illustrates the extent of his success; this was one of the most desirable addresses in Margate and was famed for its 'uniform range of handsome houses' and 'pretty seaside view'.[1] The family continued to prosper after William's birth when Thomas took ownership of the White Hart, one of Margate's more popular hotels. Nestled on the seafront along the bustling Marine Parade, the White Hart boasted extensive sea views and a steady supply of genteel patrons. While managing the hotel, Thomas continued to play a role in building works around Margate. In 1809, for example, he was involved in the rebuilding of Margate Pier after it had been battered by storms the previous year. He suggested the outer edge of the Pier be raised to provide a promenade for visitors and this idea was quickly adopted, earning Thomas great praise around the town and the reputation as a 'most intelligent builder'.[2]

When Thomas died in October 1823, William took over as manager of the White Hart. Though the hotel continued to thrive, William felt a pull in a different direction and, in 1825, entered a competition to design a new church in Margate. It was probably his father's influence and success that had introduced William to the idea of working as an architect and despite his inexperience, he possessed a natural talent for it. Of the twenty-four plans received by Reverend Baylay and Her Majesty's Commissioners, it was William's that won them over. Construction on the new church began straightaway and a procession through the town marked the laying of the foundation stone in September 1825. Here, William Edmunds rubbed shoulders with the Archbishop of Canterbury and the MP for Kent, Sir Edward Knatchbull.[3] This was high praise for the son of a carpenter and the beginning of an exciting career for the young architect.

The Holy Trinity Church came in several thousand pounds over budget but its beauty and splendour deflected any negative press from William. Before the church was completed in 1829, William had several more projects in the pipeline. He designed the Margate light house in 1828 and then Droit House, the offices of the Pier and Harbour Company.[4] In his next project, William designed Levey's Bazaar, the entrance to the town's main shopping boulevard. His plan featured a spacious layout and an 'elegant Grecian archway' that emphasised William's flair for design and his versatility as an architect. Levey's was an instant hit with Margate's genteel visitors and quickly became the most fashionable place in town to promenade.[5]

William's success in these early projects not only made him one of the county's great designers but also one of the most desirable bachelors in Margate. William offered everything a nineteenth century bride could want: he was young, energetic, financially stable and well-respected in his community. Exactly how and when he met his bride-to-be is unknown but he married Ann Christiana Burn on New Year's Day in 1828. Born on February 2 1800, in Maidstone to the now-deceased Major John Burn, of the Royal Marines, and his wife, Ann.

Following in the footsteps of William's father, the pair set up home in Hawley Square. They moved into number 16 in the north-east corner of the square and next door to the famous Theatre Royal. Ann fell pregnant straightaway and delivered the couple's first child, Christiana, in September 1828. Her birth was announced in *The Times* (though she was incorrectly described as a boy) and she was baptised on October 3 1828. Over the next four years, Ann and William welcomed a further three children into the family: William, baptised in September 1829; Mary, baptised in April 1832; and Louisa, baptised in January 1833.

Life was as good for William as it had ever been. New projects came thick and fast. In 1833 there was the Trinity Church in Dover, described as a 'beautiful Gothic structure', and the Blean Union Workhouse in Herne two years later.[6] Although William was embroiled in a scandal in 1836 with one of his employers, the Margate Pier and Harbour Company, he was quickly vindicated. According to the proprietor and one of the directors, William had forged an invoice for stone, amounting to £305, and pocketed the money. Fortunately, the stone appeared shortly after and the charge against him dropped before any lasting damage to his reputation could be done. At a meeting in January 1837, the company publicly acknowledged their support for William when the proprietors 'expressed their satisfactions at the explanations given by Mr Edmunds and at the efficient manner in which he discharges his duties'.[7]

The swift resolution of the Pier and Harbour Company scandal ensured that William continued to work on high-profile projects over the next few years. In 1838 he oversaw the remodelling of the Kent and Canterbury hospital and, in the following year, he designed a pavilion at Dover. But this was no ordinary pavilion: it was to be specially erected for a banquet in honour of Arthur Wellesley, Duke of Wellington.

Aside from his roles in the armed forces and in central government, Wellington also acted as Lord Warden of the Cinque Ports and took a particular interest in Dover and its harbour. The banquet celebrated this ceremonial role and demonstrated the public's regard for the aging duke. According to the *New Dover Guide*, this "magnificent Pavilion" covered an area of over 20,000 feet and could accommodate 2,250 guests.[8] The banquet was a great success: William's extravagant designs were highly praised by local and national press and he considered this project to be the highlight of his career.

Amid the accomplishments of William's working life, however, tragedy struck his nearest and dearest. In April 1833 Ann delivered the couple's fifth child, Frederick Thomas Edmunds. He lived for only sixteen months and was buried on August 8 1834. In the following autumn, another child, Ellen, was born but she died three months later and was buried in December 1835. The death registers do not reveal the cause of death for either Frederick or Ellen. Losing two children in two years must have been devastating for the family and Ann did not bear another child for six years. Arthur Burn Edmunds made his safe arrival into the world in October 1841. He was a healthy baby who showed no signs of serious illness but there would be no more children after him.

Although family life was joyous once again, William's career had taken an unexpected turn. In 1840 the Margate Pier and Harbour Company, for whom William worked as a surveyor, halved his annual salary to £100. Not long after, another of William's employers, the Margate Paving and Lighting Commission, followed suit and slashed his salary from £84 per annum to £60. William's employers were keen to point out that this reduction was not a result of his performance claiming instead that it was a necessary cutback as the companies underwent a programme of reform. [9] This loss of earnings did not reduce the Edmunds to a state of poverty: a typical income for the urban middle class in this period ranged anywhere from £100 per annum to £300.[10] William's salary was also bolstered by rent from a house that the couple owned on Fort Crescent, a pretty row of terraced houses along Margate's seafront. The house had been tenanted since 1828 but before Arthur's first birthday, in 1842, the lease expired and the property fell vacant. Keen to maintain this second income, William advertised the property straightaway and described the house as being 'in perfect repair' and 'in every way calculated to receive a respectable family'. Despite its good condition and prime location, William could not find neither a tenant nor buyer. He placed a second advert in *The Times* in April[11] and testimony from Ann in the 1870s reveals that a buyer soon came forward.[12] A deal to sell the house was then agreed in principle but fell through shortly after and negotiations were not renewed. To make matters worse, there is no record of William working after 1840 when he designed the pavilion at Dover.[13] This abrupt end to his career suggests that William had begun to display symptoms of ill-health, those that would later be diagnosed as general paralysis of the insane. For now, they battled through these financial hardships and made the most of the resources at their disposal.

It fell to Ann to take charge of these resources and to oversee the day-to-day running of the Edmunds household. Like other middle-class wives of the Victorian period, Ann was regarded as the 'architect of home'[14] and was in charge of all matters relating to the domestic sphere, from managing the accounts and ordering household supplies, to doing housework and caring for the children. Meeting these domestic demands was no mean feat and, like so many of her fellow wives, Ann employed a number of servants to help with her duties. In fact, by the mid-nineteenth century, three-quarters of all middle-class households employed at least one servant,[15] and the census return from 1841 shows that the Edmunds had three in their employ: Hannah Minter, Susan Nash and Margaret Jones. Though the Edmunds paid approximately £18 per year[16] for their services, a relatively high sum, the assistance that these ladies provided around the home was invaluable. This is especially true for Ann who could now delegate many of the domestic tasks, like cooking, cleaning and laundry, to the servants, rather than do them all herself. It would be wrong, however, to assume that this situation enabled Ann to live as a lady of leisure. With no nurse-maid in the house, Ann spent much of her time attending to the needs of her children and was tasked specifically with their moral, spiritual and physical development. She provided the first lessons in reading, writing, arithmetic and religion, and kept journals to mark milestones and track the progress of each child.[17] This close supervision continued until the age of 9 or 10, when the formal education of middle-class children commonly began.

When the census was taken in 1841, the only children at home were Mary, Louisa and Arthur. The two eldest children, Christiana and William, now aged 12 and 11, had moved on to the next stage in their education and had been enrolled at private boarding schools. William was already in his second year as a boarder at the King's School in Canterbury, having started a few days before his tenth birthday in 1839. Life at King's was very different to the life he had known at home. The focus was to mould William into a gentleman and prepare him for entrance into a university, and later, into a respectable profession. To do this, public schools relied heavily on strict discipline, on traditional subjects like Latin and Greek, and on team games designed to instil a sense of manliness and toughness. Fortunately, William thrived in his new surroundings and was elected a King's Scholar within his first year. This new status enabled William to receive his classical tuition free of charge for up to four years, though he still had to pay four guineas per term for his lessons in writing, arithmetic and mathematics. There were also costs for boarding and additional subjects, including French, German, drawing and fencing. Despite the high costs of his education, his records show that he stayed at King's until the midsummer term of 1842.[18]

While William learned the basics of being a gentlemen at Canterbury, his elder sister, Christiana, was sent to board at Mount Albion House, an 'establishment for ladies' in Ramsgate. The focus and scope of Christiana's education was markedly different to that of her brother's: it was not about sending her into the world to master a profession but rather about protecting her from its potentially corrupting influences. This is immediately evident in the decision to send Christiana to Ramsgate, as schools by the sea were considered healthier and more morally wholesome than those in the cities. Fortunately, Mount Albion House was nestled in a quiet, respectable street near the harbour and not too close to the hustle and bustle of the main town. This was not a purpose built school like King's but a residential property that belonged to its headmistresses, Miss Angelina Charriere and Miss Marianna Fisher. This was a common set-up for girls' boarding schools in the early Victorian period because it offered a more intimate and homely environment, ideal for training the next generations of wives and mothers.

Mount Albion House was not the only private school for girls in Ramsgate or even in this quiet street called Chapel Place. There was Miss Read's, Miss Evans', and Miss Saffery's, all on the same row. There was even a dancing master, just next door. All of these schools had resident pupils at the time of the census in 1841 but its twenty-two pupils suggests that Mount Albion House was the more popular choice. The school was well-equipped to meet the needs of so many young girls and perhaps this contributed to its popularity. Aside from the two headmistresses, there were two full-time teachers, Miss Caroline Turrion and Miss Veronica Venetozza, alongside three servants to carry out the domestic chores. Beyond these few facts, very little is known about the history or the day-to-day running of Mount Albion House. There is no official paper trail to follow as the school did not require a licence to operate and any material that might have survived was destroyed by a fire at Ramsgate Library in 2004. As a result, it is impossible to know for certain when Christiana entered Mount Albion House but she was in residence by the time of her thirteenth birthday. It was common in this period for girls to board for a year or two, as a sort of rite of passage into womanhood, but there were frequent cases when girls stayed in school for longer periods. These cases included girls who had been orphaned, for example, were deemed unmanageable by their parents, or, for whatever reason, were unable to live at home with their family. The wide variation in ages at the time of the census suggests that Christiana may have boarded with girls in such a situation but the high cost of girls' education in this period created a significant financial responsibility for their families. The cost of a private education at an establishment like Mount Albion House averaged £130 per annum,[19] equivalent to over £7,000 today, and some of the more fashionable schools charged even more. The Irish writer and reformer, Francis Power Cobbe, spent two years at one such school in Brighton in the 1830s. The cost of educating the young Frances at the home of Miss Runciman and Miss Roberts amounted to a staggering £1,000, close to £60,000 in modern currency. This consisted of a nominal fee of between £120 and £130 per annum while the rest came from extras that included a private bedroom and harp lessons. In her autobiography, Frances paints a bleak picture of her time in Brighton. If she expected to receive a well-rounded education, then she was quickly disappointed. Miss Runciman and Miss Roberts were not in the business of equipping young ladies with the skills for a career outside the home, as Frances recalled:

> *That a pupil in that school should ever become an artist, or an authoress, would have been looked upon … as a deplorable dereliction. Not that which was good in itself or useful to the community, or even that which would be delightful to ourselves, but that which would make us admired in society, was the raison d'etre of each requirement.*[20]

This sentiment was echoed by the science writer, Mary Somerville, who attended a private boarding school in the Scottish coastal town of Musselburgh. Miss Primrose's school was so expensive that Mary spent only one year there but, like Frances, she found the quality and depth of teaching to be seriously lacking. Within a few days of her arrival, she was encased in a steel busk designed to improve her posture and, in this 'constrained state', she was taught to learn and recite pages of the dictionary as well as the basics of English and French grammar. Unsurprisingly, Mary found this to be 'extremely tedious and inefficient'.[21] Similarly, Frances spent much of her school day learning the pages of textbooks by heart. In her first class at Miss Runciman's and Miss Robert's, she committed to memory no less than thirteen pages of a history book. Even worse, she would have to recite scores of English and French verbs on her weekly promenade around the neighbouring terraces.[22]

As dull and pointless as these lessons may have seemed, they were part of a set of accomplishments that formed the basis of the boarding school curriculum. These accomplishments transformed a girl into a lady, in the same way that the Classics came to define the Victorian gentleman. Learning French, English grammar and good posture, however, were not the only accomplishments that these young girls had to master. For Frances, several hours of each day were devoted to singing and learning an instrument, both of which were charged as an extra and were expected to be mastered even if the girls had 'no music in their souls' or 'voices in their throats'.[23] Frances was also attended daily by a dancing master, Madame Michaud, who schooled her in every dance practiced in England and every national dance in Europe. If this wasn't tiring enough, after dancing came a callisthenic lesson in which she performed a series of exercises with poles and dumbbells to improve and enhance her figure.[24]

There was little time for leisure amid these countless hours of lessons. Outside of the accomplishments, Frances spent hours in prayer, at Bible study and Church[25] to develop a strong sense of morality and piety. Religion played a central role in school and we can assume that much of Christiana's life at Mount Albion House involved similar lessons and regular attendance at Church. When free time did occur, it was closely supervised by teachers who sought to root out any potentially negative influences and encourage the girls' purity and modesty. Many private schools forbade pupils to read newspapers, for example, or to show any interest in masculine subjects, such as politics and economics. Some establishments even prevented girls from writing letters to anyone other than their parents.[26] When rules were broken, headmistresses reacted quickly and harshly. At Brighton, after being 'solemnly scolded', Frances recalled a number of girls being 'obliged to sit for hours ... like naughty babies, with their faces to the walls'.[27]

It is hardly surprising that Frances and Mary looked back on their time at private school negatively and felt that it had been of little academic worth. Frances so hated her time in Brighton that she could remember those 'solitary hours of first emancipation' vividly, even in her later years.[28] We can only wonder if Christiana felt the same way and if the strict routine and the hours of dancing, singing and French left her feeling physically and emotionally drained. It is likely that Christiana left Mount Albion House in 1842, as custom dictated, and returned to the family home in Margate. Unlike her brother, these brief years at boarding school marked the beginning and the end of Christiana's formal education. There would be no university studies or entrance into a profession. Her future was in marriage, the only truly acceptable profession for a middle-class lady[29] and Christiana, through her study of accomplishments, had already mastered all the skills she would need to secure a husband later in life. In the meantime, Christiana was reunited with her family but found the household to be quite different to the one she had left behind. She had a new sibling, Arthur, and her younger sisters, Louisa and Mary, were about to enrol at boarding school, perhaps also at Mount Albion House. The biggest change of all, however, was in her father. He had started to behave very strangely, he wasn't working anymore and rarely left the house. Christiana noticed the stress that this behaviour placed on her mother but neither appreciated the full extent of his illness, nor could they have predicted the tragedy that lay just around the corner.

Chapter Two

"Where Insanity Has Prevailed"

B y the summer of 1843, William Edmunds' strange behaviour had become too much for his family to bear. He raved about owning 'millions of money' and was prone to spontaneous, violent outbursts. After consulting with the family doctor, whom William attempted to knock down with a ruler,[1] Ann accepted that it was time to remove her husband from the family home and place him in the care of a psychiatrist. This was a major decision but one that she hoped would cure him of his obvious insanity.

Residential care for a person deemed to be insane depended primarily on his financial background. The majority of England's lunatics were paupers, defined as people unable to pay for their own care and who were instead confined at the expense of the parish. Paupers were confined in a number of places, from the lunatic ward of the local workhouse, to publicly-funded hospitals and even gaols. As the number of pauper lunatics increased over the late-eighteenth and early-nineteenth centuries, the pressure on these resources intensified and the government responded with the County Asylum Act of 1808. This Act encouraged counties across England and Wales to create purpose-built asylums for the care of pauper lunatics. This was not a compulsory recommendation, however, and many counties were slow to respond: by the mid-century, there were only fourteen county asylums in operation. William's home county, Kent, had opened an asylum in 1833 at Barming Heath, near Maidstone, but it was plagued by overcrowding, despite twice extending the building.

In contrast to pauper lunatics were private patients, the men and women who were able to meet the cost of their own residential care. These patients, like William Edmunds, were welcomed by the county asylums but there was a consensus among the medical profession that people of the middle and upper classes should not be placed alongside their social inferiors. According to William Browne, the physician and superintendent of the Montrose Asylum:

To strip a man suddenly, and for no reason that he can comprehend of, of all the luxuries and elegances to which he has been accustomed, and expose him to the bald simplicity and meagreness observed in establishments for the insane, would overthrow a tottering mind, and totally crush one that has already been weakened.[2]

Fortunately, an alternative to the county asylum came into existence at the end of the eighteenth century. This was the private madhouse, a profit-making business which provided residential treatment for a weekly fee. The growth in this 'trade in lunacy' was significant: the number of private madhouses in England and Wales more than trebled between 1800 and 1845. The quality of care provided by many of these institutions, however, was notoriously poor and they were often the focus of abuse scandals and tales of horror. Writing in 1837, William Browne wrote that lunatics were 'left to linger out a lifetime of misery, without any rational attempt at treatment, without employment, without a glimpse of happiness, or a hope of liberation'.[3] Though Browne's words were based on observations made at the end of the eighteenth century, the conditions in many of the country's private madhouses were slow to change, despite a growing public awareness of the need for reform. For example, the Commissioners in Lunacy, tasked with the inspection and improvement of asylums, reported that dirty, cramped conditions and the use of restraint remained a feature of asylum care as late as the 1840s.[4]

Of course, not all private madhouses operated in such a manner and William Edmunds was in no danger of living in such conditions. There were a number of private madhouses that catered almost exclusively to middle and upper-class patients, combining psychiatric care with all the comforts and amenities of a genteel house, such as a music room, aviary and horse and carriage. They were often advertised as a 'lodge' or 'retreat' and generally admitted a small number of patients. One such institution was Southall Park, a small, private madhouse on the outskirts of London which issued the following handbill in 1839:

> *For any Lady or Gentleman whose mental state may require a separation from their immediate friends and connexions ... The House is within a cheerful view of the road, but sufficiently distant from it to be free from any interruption or annoyances from the passengers ... But the principal advantages to be afforded are the domestic association and family union, which are invariably kept up with the inmates.*[5]

Perhaps after seeing this handbill, Ann decided that Southall Park would become William's home for the foreseeable future. This former mansion had been converted to an asylum by Sir William C. Ellis and his wife, Mildred, in 1838. The couple had worked together at the West Riding Asylum in Wakefield and later at Hanwell, the county asylum for Middlesex. This husband and wife team pioneered the humane treatment of lunatics and developed the 'Great Principle of Therapeutic Employment', where patients participated in work as part of their recovery. This idea was so influential that William was rewarded with a knighthood. The couple were also devout Quakers who provided daily religious instruction to their patients and encouraged Church attendance on Sundays. But less than one year after opening Southall Park, William died suddenly from dropsy but Mildred was determined to maintain the good work that she and her husband had started. She continued to work as the asylum's matron under Southall Park's new owner, Dr John Burdett Steward, a Cambridge-educated physician, and fellow owner George Wythe Daniel, a surgeon from Bristol and relative newcomer to the profession, having qualified in 1840, a few months after William Ellis's death.

The process of committing William to Southall Park was relatively straightforward. Under the 1828 Act to Regulate the Care and Treatment of Insane Persons in England, or Madhouse Act, a person could only be detained on the production of two medical certificates of lunacy that had each been signed by a different doctor. This law also required a family member to fill out a lunacy order. Once this paperwork was completed, the next step was to escort William Edmunds to Southall Park. This took place in August 1843 and William did not go without a fight. According to Ann, he had to be placed in a straitjacket and carried out of the family home by two attendants.[6] To see her father confined in such a manner must have been a traumatic experience for Christiana. Now 15-years-old, she was aware of the severity of his illness and, in all probability, of the social and financial consequences of his confinement. Like her mother, her only option was to hope that the treatment was successful and that the family could be quickly reunited.

It was Dr Steward who assessed William on his arrival at Southall Park. Based on his observations, he found William to be a 'dangerous lunatic' and later testified that the 'exciting cause of the malady was the loss of the sale of a house'.[7] This was the house in Fort Crescent that William and Ann had unsuccessfully tried to sell in the spring of 1842. Whether Dr Steward heard this directly from William is unknown but it demonstrates the impact of this event on William's state of mind and gives a clear indication of when he began to display the symptoms of mental illness. Categorised as a dangerous lunatic, it was necessary to have two attendants to care for William on a daily basis and he may have also been separated from the other patients. There are no surviving records relating to the weekly cost of his boarding and care at Southall

Park but data from similar institutions shows wide variations, from fifteen shillings to two guineas per week, approximately £50 to £120 per week in modern currency. The price depended primarily on the type of accommodation required: at Droitwich Asylum, for example, a bed on a ward with access to a court for 'air and exercise' cost one guinea per week but doubled if the patient lodged in a private apartment.[8] If William was boarded separately from the other patients, presumably in an attempt to curtail his violent outbursts then we can assume that his care cost at least one guinea per week. This was a considerable expense to a family who had just lost its breadwinner. With no adult male to take his place, Ann and the children were now reliant on savings and investments while they waited on William's recovery and return to the family home.

At such a high cost, it is not surprising that Ann was forced to remove William from Southall Park after only one year. He was not cured of his insanity but there was some improvement in his condition, though his return to Margate was bittersweet. He spent his first night at home in the family's wine cellar and his fondness for alcohol, which had been noted by Dr Steward,[9] served only to aggravate the symptoms of his condition. This intemperance made it almost impossible for William to live at home with his family and within eight months, he was confined to an asylum for the second time. He did not return to Southall Park but was instead admitted to Peckham House in March 1845, another private madhouse in London.

On the surface, Peckham House was every bit as genteel as Southall Park. In 1843, Peter Armstrong, a co-proprietor and resident physician, published the following advertisement in *The Times*:

The house is delightfully situated on the road leading from Camberwell to Peckham, three miles south of London, where the air is well-known for its mildness and salubrity. The grounds, which are extensive, are laid out with great taste, and consist of six separate airing grounds,

independent of lawn, gardens and meadow ... Mr and Mrs Armstrong
tend to the domestic arrangements, who give their constant attention
to its management ... together with the mildest treatment which their
unfortunate situation requires.[10]

The grounds and internal accommodation of Peckham House
were certainly an attractive feature and both were praised by the
Commissioners in Lunacy during a visit to the asylum in 1844.[11]
Like Southall Park, Peckham House was a former mansion that had
been converted to an asylum in 1826 but was considerably larger and
catered to a much wider clientele. In 1844, for example, there were 251
patients, 'drawn from all classes of society – from the pauper inmate to
the titled dame',[12] and though the two classes of patient lived separately,
Peckham House had come under scrutiny by the Commissioners in
Lunacy in the year prior to William's admission:

In March (1844) ... two beds for private patients objected to. Deficiency
of spoons and cans for patients at dinner, noticed. In November, two
rooms found offensive.[13]

The Commissioners returned to Peckham House in May 1845, two
months after William's admission, and complained that the male
infirmary was without a fireplace. They returned again on 20 July to
find a number of complaints against staff being investigated, one of
which involved an allegation of violence against a female inmate. The
nurse in question was dismissed[14] but these criticisms demonstrate
how different life had become for William, after having lived in
relative luxury at Southall Park. The fact that he was confined in such
an institution, living among paupers and criminals, also illustrates the
financial hardships now faced by the Edmunds family.

Peckham House may not have provided the best accommodation
or diet but its resident physician, Dr James Hill, had implemented a

progressive treatment regime that emphasised care and compassion over the violence and coercion that once dominated English asylums. Hill was inspired by a reform movement that had slowly gained momentum over the previous half century and revolutionised the treatment of the mentally ill. This movement began in 1796 when William Tuke opened a small, private asylum in York called the Retreat. Tuke had no medical or psychiatric training but had been spurred into action after witnessing first-hand the poor treatment of the mentally ill in asylums across the country. In a visit to St Luke's Hospital, for example, he saw a naked woman lying in dirty straw and chained to a wall. This image so haunted Tuke that he became determined to found his own sanctuary for the insane and did not stop until it admitted its first patients in 1796.[15]

Tuke was a devout Quaker who modelled the Retreat on non-violence and equality, the defining principles of his faith. In keeping with Quaker tradition, he referred to staff and patients as 'friends' and everyone came together on a daily basis for meals and prayer. In this environment of familial intimacy, he treated patients on an individual basis, used physical restraint sparingly and encouraged participation in meaningful activities, like arts, crafts and simple tasks on the Retreat's farm.[16] This new style of patient care was termed 'moral treatment' and was unlike anything that had been seen in England's asylums before. Tuke worked hard to demonstrate the efficacy of moral treatment and to show that his patients truly benefited from a kinder, more gentle approach. In 1813, he instructed his grandson, Samuel, to publish a complete outline of the Retreat's principles and practices in an attempt to convince others of the advantages of his model.

Despite Tuke's efforts, moral treatment was not universally adopted by asylum physicians. Many still believed that physical restraint, using manacles, chains and straitjackets, was a necessary tool in the treatment of the mentally ill, particularly with patients prone to violence and anger. Tuke did, however, inspire a number of physicians to implement his moral treatment and some even dispensed of mechanical restraint completely. We can see moral treatment in action during William's confinement at Southall Park, where patients could walk in the grounds and enjoy music and the arts. These principles also inspired John Conolly, a physician from Lincolnshire who rose to become the superintendent of the Hanwell County Asylum in Middlesex in 1839 but Conolly took moral treatment one step further than Ellis and his wife by completely eliminating the use of mechanical restraint at his asylum, despite strong opposition, both locally and nationally.

Like Tuke, Conolly believed that the mentally ill needed comfort and kindness to get better. In his book, *The Treatment of the Insane Without Mechanical Restraint*, Conolly provides ample case studies that demonstrate the effectiveness of the moral system. In one such example, concerning a cavalry officer who had spent years under restraint in another institution, we see some of his methods at work:

[the patient] *appeared to be surprised when shown into a well-furnished room, and quite astonished when he saw a comfortable dinner before him, and when his tea was decently served in the evening. Patients who have been so negligently cared for almost always improve when thus respectfully and kindly treated. They make an effort to conform to the decent habits of the house; are more careful to be cleanly when their dress is no longer the dress of a beggar; and become civil and even courteous in their demeanour. The violent conduct which caused them to be fastened in restraints ... disappears amongst the comforts of their new and better abode.*[17]

By mid-century, support for moral treatment had grown considerably and written accounts collected by the Commissioners in Lunacy show that Dr Hill was heavily influenced by its philosophy and practices. Like them, Dr Hill kept his asylum clean, bright and well-ventilated, to promote a feeling of cheerfulness on the wards. He ensured that all patients received a bath at least once a week and were dressed in clean clothes made only from flannel, to ensure they stayed 'comfortably warm'.[18]

Like the Retreat, Dr Hill provided his patients with access to a wide range of activities and distractions, from books and dominoes to music and dancing. He encouraged his patients to be outside as much as possible and believed that employment was an effective cure for all forms of mental illness. It is interesting to note that Peckham House maintained the gendered nature of work that existed in the wider society: women were engaged in needlework and laundry while men were employed on the asylum's farm or in a trade.[19] William was likely employed in the early days of his stay at Peckham House when he was still strong enough to engage in physical tasks, but it is doubtful that this continued once he had entered the latter stages of general paralysis.

Although there was no cure for William's condition, advocates of moral management had a number of remedies for general paralysis at their disposal. Asylum physicians had once treated general paralysis with mercury but Conolly had disregarded such medicines on the grounds that they continually failed to bring about a recovery.[20] Dr Hill shared Conolly's belief that bloodletting, with leeches applied to the temples or behind the ears, was a more effective alternative for general paralysis because it kept the head from overheating. Dr Hill also used a warm bath, usually for thirty minutes, to soothe patients like William during episodes of mania and often combined the treatment with a sedative in extreme cases of excitement.[21] The advocates of moral treatment had also outlawed the use of the cold bath, the practice of immersing a patient into ice cold water. In previous decades, many physicians believed that the cold bath could shock a patient's brain into recovery but, in reality, it was often used by asylum attendants to punish bad behaviour. Dr Hill was fiercely against such brutality and told the Commissioners in Lunacy that he did not allow a patient to be bathed by an attendant without his express permission. He did, however, admit to using the cold bath as a 'general tonic' in hot, summer weather.[22]

The diet of his patients was another area of great importance to Dr Hill and he recommended that food be 'nutritious in quality' and 'ample in quantity'. He prescribed daily variations in the meat and vegetables offered to patients and warned against liquid foods, like soup, which were 'very apt to produce diarrhoea'.[23] Ample amounts of solid food, however, often caused constipation and Dr Hill gave William a number of mild aperients to combat this, including rhubarb mixed with cream of tartar.[24]

Despite his efforts, Dr Hill knew that he could not cure William's condition, as he explained to the Commissioners in Lunacy: 'by great care the disease may be retarded in its progress; but I have never met with a case of recovery'.[25] William Edmunds lived for less than two years at Peckham House and died on 15 March 1847. Two days later, his passing was announced in the *Kentish Gazette* but without any reference to the cause or place in which he died.[26] William's body was not returned to his home town for burial but was instead interred in Kensall Green cemetery in London. This was one of the finest cemeteries in Victorian London and notable as the resting place of some of the era's most talented and respected artists, scientists and politicians. This was a fitting tribute to William's glowing architectural career which had ended so suddenly and in such tragic circumstances.

As William's family slowly came to terms with his death, they also had to deal with the enormous stigma attached to the manner in which he died. This stigma affected every person who died in the asylum and was, in part, a result of the perceived causes of insanity. In the nineteenth century, it was widely accepted that insanity could be trigged by any number of moral or physical causes. The moral causes of insanity might include poverty and financial worry, domestic problems and jealousy, while the physical causes ranged from menstruation and childbirth to masturbation and alcoholism. According to the physician, James Cowles Prichard, these feelings or experiences placed stress on the nervous system and interfered with the brain's proper functioning. When this occurred, there was a very real possibility that insanity could follow.[27] As a result of this thinking, insanity came to be associated with people of low moral character, with those who drank too much or allowed themselves to be governed by intense feelings. It became easy to feel prejudice towards such people because they lacked the virtues, like modesty, self-control and temperance, which were so highly-prized in the mid-nineteenth century.

Another reason for this social stigma came from the well-known and widely-accepted idea that insanity ran in families. This was based on the premise that a child inherited not only the 'inborn attributes' of its parents, but also the sum of their 'experiences, diseases, achievements, accidents and transgressions'.[28] If a parent became insane through alcoholism, for example, then it followed that his child would likely succumb to alcoholism, or a similar addiction, at some point in his or her life. Prichard summed it up succinctly: 'It seems probable that any cause which tends to produce enervation and debility in parents will have an effect on their offspring'.[29] This notion of 'hereditary insanity' was often cited by medical writers as a leading cause of madness among asylum inmates, though there was some disagreement about its prevalence. For example, George Man Burrows, the owner of the Retreat at Clapham, claimed that 85 per cent of his patients were the victims of a hereditary taint in 1828.[30] Conversely, of the 212 curable patients admitted to the Bethlem Royal Hospital in 1844, only nine males and seventeen females were diagnosed with hereditary insanity.[31] Despite such statistical variation, medical writers believed that heredity posed a very real threat to the nation's sanity. Unsurprisingly, these fears permeated more popular forms of literature, particularly those relating to marriage and procreation. This article published in the *Literary Gazette* in 1827 demonstrates how embedded in society this attitude became:

What has been advanced is sufficient to show the vital importance of inquiring into the state of every family, as far as hereditary predisposition is concerned ... Parents and guardians ... should be informed that an alliance with a family where insanity has prevailed, ought to be prohibited.[32]

The taint of hereditary madness had serious implications for the young Christiana. She was 19-years-old at the time of her father's death and on the cusp of womanhood. Around the age of 18, many middle-class girls 'came out' into society in a rite of passage that demonstrated their eligibility for romance and courtship. In wealthier middle-class families, coming out was marked by a ball or party but there were less extravagant ways of marking this occasion too, like putting up their hair and wearing longer skirts. Once the occasion had been marked, Christiana would be allowed to participate in her parents' social circle and accompany them on visits and to dinner parties.[33] As her coming out coincided with her father's confinement in Peckham House, the reality for Christiana was very different from this idealised version. There would be no ball in her honour, no social calls or line of suitors at her door. Christiana and her family were the victims of intense speculation, even if they were able to conceal the truth surrounding his mysterious disappearance from public life. His sudden death only exacerbated the rumours and the gossip. Christiana's thoughts inevitably turned to her future and what it might hold. She had been groomed for marriage and a life of domesticity but the taint on her family's reputation put everything in jeopardy. After all, what kind of man, if any, would want to marry the daughter of a lunatic?

In the meantime there were practical matters to attend to. One month after William's death, on 14 April, 1847, William's will was proved before the court of probate and she received a one-off payment of £100 towards the family's maintenance. Under the terms of the will, Ann received all of her husband's personal possessions to do with as she pleased. A few weeks later, the following advertisement appeared in the *Kentish Gazette*:[34]

The contents of the house demonstrate the wealth and luxury in which the family had once lived and included mahogany furniture, valuable oil paintings and a piano. Every household item, from the bronze tea urn to the curtains and carpets, was to be sold in preparation for new tenants in Hawley Square.[35] At first glance, it appears that Ann held this auction because the family were in need of money, but under the terms of William's will, Ann would receive an annual allowance for the rest of her life or until she remarried, should she wish to take another husband. With this in mind, it is more likely that she sought a fresh start for herself and her children. Once the sale of goods was completed on 2 June, Ann and her children were free to set up in their new home. They did not stay in Margate but instead chose to make a fresh start in a new town, away from the gossip and scandal that dogged William's death. Their destination was Canterbury, less than twenty miles away from Margate but far enough, they hoped, from the taint of William's madness.

Chapter Three

"A Creature of Leisure"

The Edmunds' sudden departure from Margate coincides with their brief disappearance from public record and perhaps demonstrates their successful integration into Canterbury society. The city certainly had much to offer its newest residents: by the mid-nineteenth century, Canterbury was a bustling place with a population of over 10,000 and its historical cathedral made it one of the most popular tourist destinations in the country. Its economy was thriving too, with strong brewing and corn-milling industries which boosted local commerce and attracted large numbers of migrant workers to the area.[1] When the family reappear in the spring of 1851, they are living in very different circumstances to those in Margate. They no longer live amongst the lawyers and physicians of Hawley Square, and the servants they had once depended upon have been dismissed. The Edmunds are living in the upstairs of 21 St George's Street, a house in the heart of the city. Downstairs lives James Nash, his wife and young family, who came to Canterbury from Hampshire in 1840. Nash was a brush-maker, hat and basket manufacturer who operated a successful business from his shop in the front of the house.

While the Edmunds adapted to these changes in their environment, there were great changes in the structure of the household. Shortly after the family's arrival in Canterbury, the eldest son, William, left the city and headed to university in London to study medicine. He showed great talent in the subject and was admitted to the Royal College of Surgeons in 1852. He worked briefly as a surgeon in the army before emigrating to South Africa to start a new life in 1854. He took with him his new wife, Georgiana Harrington, a 36-year-old widow from Chelsea, whom he married weeks before leaving the country. William's career had been financed by his late father who had set up a trust fund for each of his children. For his sons, he bequeathed an unspecified amount to meet the cost of their education, entrance into a profession and general 'advancement in the world'.[2] But for his daughters, William envisaged a very different life and had not provided financial support for Christiana, Louisa or Mary to enter into a profession. He subscribed to the view that marriage was the only truly acceptable path for a young lady and bequeathed to each daughter one-half of her trust fund on the day of her wedding.[3] At the time of the census in 1851, Christiana and Mary were both unmarried and living at home with their mother but Louisa had fled to London in search of a new life. Sometime before 1851 she accepted a position as a governess in the home of Nina Welsh, a merchant's wife and a native of New York, who now lived in a prestigious development in Camberwell called Champion Hill.

As a lady, Louisa was neither expected nor encouraged to work outside of the home. Victorian society idealised her as a "creature of leisure" who was completely supported by her father or husband[4] and who had no need to risk her respectability by earning a wage. Of course, this idealised image was often very different from reality and there were many ladies, like Louisa, who had no male relative on whom they could financially rely. For this reason, the Victorians came to accept the role of governess far more readily than any other profession. After all, this type of work took place inside the home and was the only profession in which being a lady was the requisite.[5]

By 1850 there were around 20,000 governesses in employment in Britain and they were tasked with educating the daughters of the some of the country's wealthiest families. The quality of teaching and variety of subjects covered varied from governess to governess, depending entirely on her skills and personal interests. Generally, a governess was expected to teach the basics, like English and arithmetic, alongside genteel accomplishments, like music and languages. She was also expected to act as a chaperone outside of the home and to provide supervision on a daily basis. At Champion Hill, Louisa had three pupils to teach: Nina's daughter, also called Nina, and her two resident nieces, Petwin and Eliza. The girls were all born in the Honduras and they ranged from 10 to 13 years old. Aside from her siblings, Louisa had no practical experience with children and it is very likely that she encountered some initial difficulties in establishing her authority. The governess's ambiguous position in the household also set the scene for conflict with her employer, and is neatly summarised by one Victorian commentator: 'the real discomfort of a governess's position in a private family arises from the fact that it is undefined. She is not a relation, not a guest, not a mistress, not a servant – but something made up of all. No one knows exactly how to treat her'.[6]

Amid this uncertainty over her status, Victorian households varied greatly in their treatment of the governess. While some employers respected and cared about their governess, there were many reported cases of disobedience, snobbery and even physical cruelty.[7] Without written records, we are left to wonder how Nina Welsh and her children treated the young Louisa and for how long she stayed with the family. But, even in the most amiable environment, working as a governess offered neither prosperity nor permanence. On average, a governess could expect to earn between £20 and £45 per year[8], depending on her level of education. This included the cost of bed and board but did not cover any incidental expenses, like laundry and medical care[9] and it was thus highly important that a governess saved what money she could. Her position came with no guarantees: she could be dismissed at any time and faced stiff competition in finding a new situation. During times of unemployment, she had only her savings on which to rely and no pension to look forward to in her retirement.[10] From 1843, the Governesses' Benevolent Institution provided assistance to those who were between jobs or who were too old or sick to work, but there was still some way to go to improve the working conditions of the Victorian governess. For Louisa, her new life presented as many challenges as the one she had left behind in Margate but she was determined to make the best of her situation and never returned to live with her family.

Back in Canterbury, Christiana had no intention of following her sister into such a profession. Since the death of her father, she had become increasingly emotional and sensitive and clung to her mother than more than ever. Ann would later report that Christiana would burst into her room at night, claiming that she had a 'fit of hysteria and could not breathe'.[11] By 1853, Ann had become so concerned with her daughter's behaviour that she sent her to London to see a doctor. He diagnosed Christiana with hysteria, one of the most commonly-experienced ailments of the Victoria era.

Hysteria was categorised as a nervous illness that affected both body and mind and created a wide-range of symptoms, including shortness of breath, muscular spasms, fainting, anxiety, irritability and insomnia. Physicians increasingly came to view hysteria as a female-only ailment because historically, the uterus had been identified as the underlying cause. Even the word *hysteria* was rooted in this idea, deriving from a Greek word that means 'that which proceeds from the uterus'. According to the Greek philosopher Plato, the uterus was an animal that roamed inside a woman's body, causing illness as it moved around. Pain in the abdomen, for example, was caused by a uterine attack on the liver, while feelings of lethargy came from the uterus squeezing the blood vessels that travelled toward the brain.[12]

The notion of a 'wandering womb' that attacked the female body persisted for centuries among physicians. It was only in the mid-nineteenth century, around the time of Christiana's diagnosis, that uterine explanations of hysteria begin to fade in prominence.[13] Some physicians went so far as to reject the very term hysteria, on the grounds that this uterine connection was unsound. One such person was Frederick Carpenter Skey, a physician specialising in hysteria, who preferred the term 'local nervous irritation'.[14] In place of the wandering womb came new ideas about the causes of hysteria and physicians became particularly interested in the menstrual cycle, for example, and began to study its impact on the hysterical woman.[15] In his *Treatise on Hysteria*, the physician, George Tate, wrote:

> *Since I have been attentive to cases of hysteria, I have never seen one, either of a simple or of a complex character, in which there did not co-exist distinct traces of a faulty menstruation. There is always some deficiency or depravity of this secretion ... I take it to be a justifiable conclusion, that this is a fundamental cause, and that our remedial means ought to be directed to that cause.*[16]

As physicians studied more closely the role of menstruation in creating hysteria, they began to see how dramatically its absence could affect a woman's state of mind. According to James Cowles Prichard, 'females ... experience a suppression of the catamenia (menstruation), followed in some instances immediately by fits of epilepsy or hysteria, the attacks of which are so sudden as to illustrate the connexion of cause and effect'.[17] What especially interested physicians, however, was how the return of menstruation could bring about symptomatic relief: 'We have already alluded to the case of a young female,' continued Prichard, 'who suddenly exclaimed that she was cured of her disorder; her catamenia had flowed spontaneously, and her restoration to sanity was the immediate consequence'.[18]

In this understanding, then, a woman's menstrual flow was characterised as an explosive, hysterical energy. This energy was primarily sexual in its nature and controlling it became the key to preventing and curing incidences of hysteria in the female population. A central problem, however, was that women had very few opportunities in which to legitimately vent this sexual energy, and, while Victorian society accepted this fact, it was not prepared to change.[19]

By adhering to the strict codes of acceptable feminine behaviour, Christiana Edmunds had unwittingly caused her own hysteria. Her chastity, modesty and devotion to domesticity, traits that were first developed at Mount Albion House, had created an energy that threatened her physical and mental health. In his famous lecture on hysteria in 1866, Julian Althaus acknowledged that this was a common problem for women of Christiana's status: '[hysteria] is frequent in the higher classes of society, in ladies, who lead an artificial life, who do nothing, whose every wish or whim is often gratified as soon as formed'. His solution to these cases of hysteria was 'real honest work' or 'the pursuance of an object in life', not in a profession, but rather 'the education of children or some charitable undertaking'.[20]

The idea that Christiana might channel her nervous energy into philanthropy was not a realistic one. On her return from London, her symptoms of hysteria had intensified and she became paralysed on one side of her body and in her feet.[21] Paralysis was a common symptom of hysteria that tended to occur after an attack of 'painful emotions'. Episodes of paralysis varied enormously in their intensity and duration among patients but physicians noticed that the left side of the body and the legs were most frequently reported.[22] During Christiana's attack of paralysis, she was attended by a surgeon called Mr Prettyman who had a number of remedies with which to treat his new patient. First of all, Prettyman had to understand and remove the root cause, or the 'painful emotion', which had caused her bout of hysteria. For Christiana, this was likely the grief she felt after the loss of her father or perhaps the family's upheaval to Canterbury in 1847. Once the root cause was identified, it was Mr Prettyman's job to 'rouse the will' of his patient by promoting her optimism and encouraging the support of those around her. He might even suggest a change of scenery or air to improve her overall mood. Next, he might focus on Christian's constitution. If she appeared pale and anaemic, he would recommend a diet rich in milk, poultry, wine and chocolate, alongside a cold sponge bath in the morning and two to three doses of iron each day. Conversely, if her complexion was ruddy, he advised bland food, saline remedies, regular warm baths and occasional blood-letting.[23]

With her diet and constitution in order, Mr Prettyman could now turn to Christiana's bodily functions, a source of much interest among physicians. He enquired about the frequency of her bowel movements and how often she passed urine. If these were not in 'proper order', he might then prescribe a course of laxatives or emetics.[24] Menstruation was considered the most important bodily function of a female patient and Christiana could expect to be questioned at length on the frequency and character of her periods. Given her diagnosis of hysteria, it is likely that her menstruation was irregular, if at all present, during her illness in 1853, and that her doctor sought to bring about its return and thus dispel her hysterical energy.

Writing in 1840, the Scottish physician, Alexander Tweedie, outlined a number of methods that could be used to induce menstruation in the hysterical woman. The first was to place leeches on the labia or thighs as the patient approached her usual time of menstruation, while also submerging her feet in a bath of mustard. If this method proved unsuccessful, Dr Tweedie recommended a single dose of a mixture made from aloe, digitalis (a foxglove) and calomel, (mercury chloride), followed by a laxative. This was to be followed by a pill containing aloe, myrrh and galbanum, a type of resin, twice daily, until menstruation returned. If both of these methods failed, Dr Tweedie turned to a guaranteed solution: the transmission of an electrical charge through the patient's pelvis to kick-start an 'evacuation'.[25]

Dr Tweedie was not the only physician to recommend the use of electricity to treat hysteria and its troublesome symptoms. In fact, electrotherapy, or galvanism as it was known, was so popular by the

1840s that there were a plethora of galvanic machines on the market. These machines contained a small battery that discharged a continuous current of electricity. A piston controlled the current's intensity and two conductors enabled the user to direct the electricity to any part of the body. Galvanic belts, worn around the patient's trunk, and even rings and ear plates became fashionable accessories in the battle against hysteria. One of galvanism's staunchest supporters was Thomas Laycock, a physician who rose to become one of era's leading voices on female nervous diseases. Like Tweedie, Laycock favoured the use of galvanism above any method of treatment but believed that hysteria was caused by the increasing immorality and sexualisation of ladies and had little do with the menstruation: 'Young females of the same age, and influenced by the same novel feelings towards the opposite sex, cannot associate together in public schools without serious risk of exciting the passions, and of being led to indulge in practices injurious to both body and mind'. As a result, 'the young female returns from school to her home, a hysterical, wayward, capricious girl; imbecile in mind, habits and pursuits; prone to hysteric paroxysms upon any unusual mental excitement'.[26]

Laycock was not alone in the view that intense sexual feelings created the symptoms of hysteria and, in expressing this opinion, he echoed ideas that were centuries old. This belief had given rise to genital massage, one of the most notorious treatments of the nineteenth century. The practice of massaging a woman to orgasm to relieve her sexual energy and thus cure her hysteria dated back to the time of Galen but was practiced on an unprecedented scale by the Victorians. In fact, the demand for this treatment was so high that it prompted the invention of the vibrator, not as a tool for sexual pleasure but as a labour-saving device for physicians.[27]

As genital massage and galvanism were so routinely used by physicians in the mid-nineteenth century, it is not unreasonable to suggest that these methods were employed as part of Christiana's treatment. Whatever the case, her treatment proved unsuccessful and she continued to experience bouts of hysteria throughout the course of her adult life. She was not the only woman in the Edmunds family to suffer either. Her sister, Louisa, was plagued by hysteria and depression as an adult, though there are no records to indicate the extent or severity of her symptoms.[28] That Louisa continued to work in London as a governess throughout the 1850s, however, suggests that she was able to conceal or control her symptoms during this period, well enough to maintain her employment.

A year or so after Christiana's visit to London, her youngest brother, Arthur, began to display some worrying symptoms. His mood became increasingly sombre, often angry, and he started to have seizures. Shortly before the onset of these symptoms, Arthur had received a blow to the head but it was not severe enough to bring about such changes, according to his mother.[29] Nevertheless, she related this incident to the family physician who diagnosed Arthur with epilepsy. This common neurological disorder is characterised by a tendency to have seizures and was first recognised by the Ancient Babylonians who believed that it was caused by an evil spirit. This supernatural explanation persisted well into the eighteenth century but by the Victorian period, the focus had changed and physicians claimed that epilepsy was the result of excessive masturbation. According to the Swiss-born physician, Samuel Auguste Tissot: 'too great a quantity of semen being lost in the natural course produces very direful effects: but they are still more dreadful, when the same quantity has been dissipated in an unnatural manner'. This view went unchallenged throughout the century, prompting the French physician, Jean Alfred Fournier, to declare that 'one of the nervous affections which onanism occasions most frequently is epilepsy … There are very few physicians who have not observed cases where it has been produced, maintained or aggravated by the practice of this pernicious habit'.[30]

The notion that excessive masturbation caused epilepsy has long been defunct but there is another possible explanation for the sudden onset of seizures in the young Arthur Edmunds and it relates to the death of his father from general paralysis in 1847. As mentioned previously, the German physicians, Esmarch and Jessen, demonstrated a causal relationship between syphilis and general paralysis in 1857, but their findings were not accepted by the medical establishment. Instead, physicians continued to argue that general paralysis was the result of environmental factors, like intemperance and promiscuity.[31] But, in 1913, the Japanese bacteriologist, Hideyo Noguchi, found syphilis in the brains of general paralysis patients,[32] thereby providing irrefutable proof of their causal relationship.

Whether William Edmunds knew he had syphilis is open to speculation because this highly contagious bacterial disease has very mild symptoms that are easy to overlook. William may not have noticed the small and painless chancre which develops in the weeks after infection or the non-itchy skin rash, weight loss and flu-like symptoms which characterise the second stage of this disease. Even if William became concerned by these symptoms, and received the proper diagnosis, there was no cure for syphilis in the nineteenth century. Doctors did, however, have a number of treatment options at their disposal, including cauterisation of the chancre or pills and potions made from mercury. The latter quickly became a popular method of choice but it was completely ineffective and came with a range of nasty side-effects, like tooth loss and gastro-intestinal problems. For bachelors, some doctors offered no treatment at all and instead advised their patients to simply wait a few years before marriage, in the belief that syphilis would eventually go away.[33] Of course, this view of syphilis is inherently flawed. When left untreated, the disease enters a latent phase in which the patients experiences no symptoms but remains contagious for the first year. Latency can last for many years before the patient reaches the third and most dangerous phase: tertiary syphilis and disorders like general paralysis of the insane. The introduction of antibiotics in the early twentieth century has rapidly reduced the number of people who reach this final phase but, for the Victorians, tertiary syphilis was a very real and very frightening possibility.

At first glance, it is tempting to conclude that William Edmunds contracted syphilis as a bachelor and infected his wife at the time of their marriage. That Ann contracted syphilis is without question because the disease is passed primarily through sexual intercourse and contraception to prevent its spread did not exist at the time of their marriage. However, contemporaries knew that procreating in the shadow of syphilis was an inherently dangerous practice and warned young couples against it:

It [syphilis] *can take such severe forms, after marriage, that not only may a wife be affected from her husband, but the children born of the marriage may suffer to a serious extent; in other words, certain private diseases of the father, that have been contracted before marriage, can be transmitted in hideous and loathsome forms to his children.*[34]

The notion that syphilis passes congenitally is correct but the Victorian wrongly identified the father as the source of infection. Observations made in the twentieth century showed that syphilis is transmitted from mother to child in utero via the placenta or on contact with maternal blood during childbirth. Not every child born to an infected mother, however, will go on to develop congenital syphilis. In fact, the rate of transmission depends on the stage of the mother's infection. According to modern studies, if she is recently infected, there is a 59 per cent chance that her baby will develop congenital syphilis but the likelihood decreases to 13 per cent chance for mothers in the more advanced phases.[35]

Children who are born with congenital syphilis often develop symptoms in the first two years of life. These symptoms, which include fever, gastroenteritis and pneumonia, can be fatal to children of at such a young age. The health of William and Ann's first four children: Christiana, William, Mary and Louisa, provides strong evidence against the idea that William contracted syphilis before his marriage in 1828. An analysis of the family tree suggests instead that William became infected around 1833, when his architectural work required his frequent absence from the family home. In this scenario, Frederick and Ellen were the first two victims of congenital syphilis in the Edmunds family and this idea is supported by the work of Max Kassovitz, a paediatrician and leading figure in the study of congenital syphilis. According to his law of 1875, congenital syphilis is defined by 'the spontaneous gradual diminution in intensity of syphilitic transmission'.[36] In other words, with each succeeding pregnancy, the effect of syphilis on a foetus will gradually decrease in intensity. This process takes around six to eight years, after which the mother is no longer infectious and therefore poses no threat to any further children.[37]

After Ellen's death, Ann did not deliver a baby for six years, a significant gap for a woman who generally birthed on a near-annual basis. It is probable, however, that she did fall pregnant during this period but succumbed to miscarriages that were not historically recorded. Modern studies have shown that women with syphilis are twelve times more likely to miscarry than those who are not infected.[38] When Ann finally delivered a baby boy in October 1841, he appeared healthy and there was cause for optimism in the family, but this is not uncommon in cases of congenital syphilis, where approximately two-thirds of children display no symptoms at birth or in the first two years of life.[39] Instead, the disease manifests later in childhood, as expressed in Kassovitz's law, and seizures are one of the most widely-reported symptoms.[40] These seizures are often accompanied by a build-up of fluid on the brain, known as hydrocephalus, which might also account for Arthur's sudden irritability and violent behaviour.[41] Whatever the case, Arthur's health was steadily deteriorating and, unbeknown to his mother, history was about to repeat itself in the Edmunds household.

Chapter Four

"Exciting the Passions"

B y 1860, Arthur's seizures and violent outbursts had become too much for his mother to bear and Ann found herself in a situation painfully reminiscent to the one she had experienced with her husband almost two decades earlier. Unable to cope with Arthur's deteriorating condition, Ann placed her son in the Royal Earlswood Asylum, a purpose-built hospital for 'idiots' near Reigate in Surrey. Earlswood was a relatively new institution, built to replace a smaller asylum called Park House, and was officially opened by Prince Albert in July 1854. Unlike other institutions for the mentally ill, Earlswood prided itself on providing its patients with opportunities for education and employment in the hope that they might become financially independent and therefore less of a burden to their families.[1] For this reason, the Board of Management prioritised the admission of children over older people, usually for a training period of five years but this could be extended to life, in more extreme cases.[2] Once admitted, patients spent half of their day in lessons and the other half learning an occupation of which there was a wide range of choice, including carpentry, plumbing, tailoring and farming.[3]

Arthur was admitted as a private patient to the Royal Earlswood in February 1860 and was described by the medical superintendent, Dr John Langdon-Down, as an 'idiot' and 'imbecile' who was suffering from epilepsy.[4] Langdon-Down had joined the Royal Earlswood in 1858, despite having no formal training or experience in mental illness and developmental disabilities. What he did have, however, was a brilliant mind, a friendly manner and a genuine enthusiasm for his new post. During his time at the Royal Earlswood, he banned all forms of punishment and restraint, introduced amusements for the patients and introduced the teaching of basic skills, like using a knife and fork, alongside vocational training. He also improved the quality of the attendants who worked there[5] in an attempt to raise the overall standard of care provided to patients. Within a few years of Langdon-Down's arrival, the Royal Earlswood's reputation was unrivalled by any other asylum in the country.

Arthur's removal to Earlswood left only his mother and Christiana at home. In 1856 Mary Edmunds had married Benjamin Edward Foreman, a clergyman, and had moved with him to Henley –on-Thames. By 1861, they had relocated to Worthing in Sussex, where Foreman worked as the incumbent of North Stoke, and had two children: Agnes Mary, born in 1858; and Ethel Burn, born in 1860. In those few short years, Christiana and her mother had moved house too: from the brush-maker's house on St George's Street, they went to Watling Street, and finally, to twenty-three Burgate Street, a confectioner's shop with accommodation above. It was here that Louisa informed her mother and sister of her engagement to Julian Watson Bradshaw, a former Navy surgeon who was now in private practice in London.

Louisa left her situation sometime before 1861 and took a new job in the home of Frederick Child, a printer, and his wife, Caroline, who lived in the St Giles area of London. Her work here was very different to Champion Hill because the children in her care were considerably younger and not at an age where education was necessary. Her three charges: Ernest, aged 4; Walter, aged 3; and Isabel, aged 2, required her constant supervision and assistance. Louisa did not stay long in St Giles, perhaps due to the demands of the children, and it is likely that she met her husband-to-be in a professional capacity, given that governesses had little free time and were generally not allowed to court while in employment. In the same year that Louisa left St Giles, Julian

Watson Bradshaw was in need of a governess because his second wife, Mary Sarah, died suddenly, leaving him with the sole responsibility of caring for his nephew, Otto, and niece, Mary. It was not unusual for love to blossom between a governess and her employer, as famously portrayed in the novel, *Jane Eyre*, and the pair were married in the winter of 1862.

From London, Julian and Louisa moved to her hometown of Margate and rented 31 Lower Marine Terrace, a pretty house facing the sea. Now the wife of a respected surgeon, Louisa did not work again and instead became the mistress of her own middle-class household. But these material comforts did not prevent repeated bouts of depression and hysteria. On one occasion, she attempted to throw herself from an upstairs window while 'in a fit' and was saved only by the quick reactions of a servant.[6] On 28 June 1867, Louisa collapsed outside of her home on Marine Terrace and died shortly after. She was only 36-years-old and died in the presence of her friend and neighbour, Eliza Stevens. Her death certificate cites menorrhagia, or heavy periods, and 'effusion and exhaustion' as the causes of her sudden demise. Evidently, Louisa suffered from some gynaecological complaint, perhaps endometriosis, and this might also explain why she bore no children during her five years of marriage; an unusual situation in an era without contraception. That she died from having a period, however, is extremely unlikely, but it is important to remember that Victorian death attributions were often vague and ambiguous, especially to modern readers.

This wasn't the only tragedy to befall the Edmunds family in the late 1860s. One year before his sister, on 11 January 1866, Arthur Edmunds died in the Royal Earlswood Asylum. The causes of his death were cited as epilepsy, a condition he had for ten years, and marasmus, a chronic state of severe malnutrition, from which he suffered for two months. Given the high standard of care in Earlswood at this time, it is unlikely that Arthur starved as a result of neglect or abuse. In fact, modern studies have shown that marasmus has a wide range of causes, including bacterial or viral infections, lactose intolerance and Crohn's disease.[7] It is also possible that a high number of seizures prevented Arthur from eating adequate food at the asylum's specified meal times. After the deaths of Arthur and Louisa, Ann and Christiana did not stay in Canterbury. For the second time, they decided to start afresh and build a new life in a new town. They headed further afield this time and left the county of Kent, heading west to East Sussex and to the seaside town of Brighton.

Like Margate, Brighton had rapidly developed in the mid-eighteenth century as a result of the popularity of sea-bathing. The man responsible for this sudden interest in the sea's medicinal properties, Dr Richard Russell, had set up his practice in the town in the 1750s, placing Brighton at the centre of this trend. While medical trends come and go, the visit of the Prince of Wales, later King George IV, to the town in 1783 guaranteed Brighton's reputation as one of the most fashionable resorts in the country.[8] George so enjoyed his visit to the town that he soon began the construction of a summer residence, the Royal Pavilion, which would become the ultimate symbol of opulence and pleasure in Regency England. As royal patronage transformed Brighton's fortunes, housing developments, businesses and attractions sprang up to meet the demands of its new wealthy clientele. By the 1820s, Brighton had become the fastest-growing town in the country and the home of the first purpose-built pleasure pier in England. Royal patronage of the town continued under George's heir, William IV (1830–1837) but Queen Victoria (1837–1901) did not share her predecessor's enthusiasm for the Royal Pavilion. She found it unsuitable for her growing family and sold it to the town of Brighton for £50,000 in 1850. This loss of patronage did not hamper Brighton's growth, however, thanks to the arrival of the railway in 1841. Brighton was now more accessible than ever and, by 1860, was welcoming by train over 250,000 people every year.[9]

By the time Christiana and her mother arrived in Brighton in 1867, the town had over 77,000 inhabitants and was at the height of its popularity. The pair rented rooms at 15 Marlborough Place, a large house in the centre of Brighton and close to the Royal Pavilion and the seafront. The house belonged to George Over, an accountant and auctioneer, and his wife, Alice, with whom Christiana and her mother became instant friends. Sometime after their arrival, the Overs introduced Christiana to Dr Charles Beard, the man who would become her physician and a major force in the course of her life. Beard worked from his home at 64 Grand Parade, just across the road from Marlborough Place, and was friendly, of good standing in the community and well-respected in his profession. Charles had studied medicine at the prestigious Trinity College, Cambridge, having enrolled there in July 1846, at the age of 18. He received his Bachelor of Medicine in 1855, his Medical Licence in 1857 and spent time as a student at St Bartholomew's Hospital in London. This was an impressive resumé and Charles had no shortage of patients when he set up his private practice in Brighton around 1861. Between tending to the town's wealthy residents, he also worked at the Sussex County Hospital and travelled frequently to the north where he became the Government Inspector of Vaccinations in the Midlands and later in the West Riding area of Yorkshire.

Very little is known about Christiana's medical history in this period but she did suffer with neuralgia, an illness possibly diagnosed by Dr Beard. Neuralgia is a condition which causes pain along the course of a nerve and commonly presents in the hands and face. In the nineteenth century, it was routinely treated with quinine and iron, a mixture which Christiana purchased from Isaac Garrett, a chemist with premises on Western Road and later on Queen's Road.[10] Neuralgia was frequently attributed to hysteria by nineteenth century physicians but whether Dr Beard knew of Christiana's previous bouts of hysteria or her trip to London in 1853 remains unknown. It is unlikely that she told him about her father and brother's deaths in the asylum, for fear that she and her mother might be socially ostracised in their new hometown.

The professional relationship between Christiana and Dr Beard soon blossomed into friendship. She listened with interest to the stories of his travels to the north and of his military escapades in Italy, back in 1860 when he had joined the British Volunteers and assisted General Garibaldi. He learned of Christiana's artistic skills and asked her to copy some anatomical drawings to hang on the walls of the Sussex County Hospital. She began writing letters to him, as many as three per week, and visited him as often as possible.[11] This attachment towards Dr Beard has been the subject of intense speculation since 1870, as contemporaries and modern writers have tried to understand the nature of their relationship. The lack of surviving evidence has made this a very difficult question to answer but the view that Christiana's case was one of unrequited love has become the consensus view. It is important to note, however, Dr Beard did not actively discourage her affections during this period. He continued to receive her letters and did not stop seeing her, either professionally or personally. At the very least, then, Dr Beard felt flattered by Christiana's attention and may have enjoyed a little flirtation. But Christiana's feelings advanced quickly into an unhealthy obsession which effected great changes in her personality and demeanour. Her landlords, George and Alice Over, were some of the first people to notice these changes. The 'ladylike, quiet and kind' woman who had arrived in Brighton just a few years earlier had been replaced by a woman consumed by her passions. The 'wildness in her look' and her edgy, excited manner made them feel uncomfortable[12] and may explain why Christiana and her mother left the house and moved elsewhere. They took rooms on the street adjacent, at 17 Gloucester Place, but the move had no impact on Christiana's relationship with Dr Beard. She continued to write to him frequently, to talk of him endlessly and to devise new means of attracting his attention. Ann became increasingly worried about

Christiana but she was powerless to alter her state of mind. Ann would later admit that she had always dreaded this time of her daughter's life and she certainly had her reasons for doing so. For a start, Christiana was 42 years old when she became consumed by her passion for Dr Beard, the same age as her father when he first displayed the symptoms of insanity.[13] In Ann's mind, this was no coincidence: it was confirmation of hereditary transmission, that dreaded biological taint which corrupted generations of a family. Even if Ann could somehow lessen her daughter's attachment to Dr Beard, there was no guarantee that she could undo the damage to Christiana's mind. But Ann could not completely lay the blame for Christiana's apparent insanity on her husband. In fact, Ann's family had its own secret history of madness which began with her own father, John Burn.

Burn was born in Rochester in Kent in the summer of 1775 and died eight years before the birth of his granddaughter, Christiana, in 1828. Burn was, perhaps, encouraged to join the Royal Marines by his own father, the great Major-General John Burn, whose memoirs and life story were posthumously published in 1840. We know far less about his son's naval career, however, and even less about his state of mind. Ann would later recall that her father was 'subject to fits' and 'quite childish' at times but this did not prevent him from maintaining his employment: he joined the Royal Marines as a Captain in 1798[14] and was promoted to the rank of Major in 1814. According to Ann, he spent his final days fastened to a chair and died 'in a fit' on October 13 1820, at the age of 45.

While insanity appears to have passed over Ann Edmunds and her six siblings, it reared its ugly head in the next generation of the family. This time it was Ellen, the daughter of Ann's older brother, John Southerden Burn, who was born in 1826. From early childhood, Ellen was described by the family as being 'quite imbecile' and had a 'weakness of intellect.'[15] Clearly she suffered from some developmental disabilities but there are no surviving medical records which detail the exact nature of her problems. When her mother died in 1847, Ellen did not stay with her father in London but was instead sent to live with various members of the Burns family and spent several years with Ann and Christiana when they lived in Canterbury.

There was likely a third reason why Ann came to fear this time of Christiana's life: she was quickly approaching her menopause, an event which Victorian doctors linked to certain mental disorders, like hysteria, melancholia, and impulsive behaviours, like drinking spirits and stealing. The famous gynaecologist, Edward Tilt, even claimed that the menopause could induce a woman to murder.[16] Because the menopause so profoundly affected a woman, Tilt and his colleagues encouraged a morally wholesome lifestyle, which included the repression of sexual feeling, until the change was over and the 'tranquillity of mind' returns.[17] This, then, was a dangerous time for Christiana but she showed no sign of relenting her quest for Dr Beard, no matter what her mother told her.

The man at the centre of Christiana's obsession, Dr Beard, also had to tread carefully but for very different reasons. He was a married man and, by entertaining or encouraging Christiana's affections, he risked not only his marriage but also his professional reputation. When he first attended Christiana in 1867, he was in his seventh year of marriage to Emily and the couple had three children: Hugh, born in 1861; Arthur, born 1863; and Emily, born 1866. Their fourth child, Frank, was born the year that he met Christiana, in 1867, and their fifth child, Edith Mary, arrived in 1869. Emily had become acquainted with Christiana through her husband and the pair had become good friends, frequently calling on each other at home, but she had no knowledge of Christiana's letters nor of her intense feelings towards her husband.

Late one evening in September 1870, while Dr Beard was away, Christiana called at his house on Grand Parade. It was not unusual for Christiana to call at Emily's house so late: in fact, Emily was glad of the company during one of her husband's many absences in London.

One of the servants showed Christiana to the drawing room, where she found Emily sitting with Miss Richardson, her deaf and elderly lodger, and Christiana explained that she had brought some chocolates from Maynard's, the confectioner, for the children, a gesture which Emily appreciated. Christiana then sat down, took out one of the chocolate creams and placed it into Emily's mouth. Emily was immediately overcome by its cold and metallic taste and had to leave the room to spit the chocolate out. Christiana offered no explanation for her actions; she simply made her excuses and left the house.

This bizarre incident left Emily feeling baffled. She was certain that the chocolate cream was responsible for the excess saliva and diarrhoea that she experienced that night but unsure if Christiana knew that the cream would cause these effects. Dr Beard returned from London later in the month and, after a few days, Emily related the strange events of that night. She had no reason to believe that Christiana harboured any ill-will towards her and was certain that the whole affair was little more than an accident. However, her husband suspected foul play immediately. After all, he knew that Christiana was in love with him and he now feared that she viewed his wife as an obstacle to their union. Dr Beard did not divulge this information to Emily but he did warn her to stay away from Christiana and her mother for the time being.

The next day, Dr Beard called at Gloucester Place to see Christiana but this was not a social visit. He had come to question her about the chocolate creams, specifically why she had attempted to poison his wife. Christiana strongly refuted his accusations, claiming that she had no intention of 'doing mischief' and that she had herself fallen ill after eating some of the same batch of chocolate creams. She craved his sympathy and understanding but he was infuriated by her denial and lack of any adequate explanation. Perhaps to force a confession, he proceeded to tell her of the spectroscope, an instrument he had recently read about which was capable of detecting poison in animal tissue, but this only heightened Christiana's indignation. She would not admit to any wrongdoing and Dr Beard had little choice but to take his leave and hope that this would be the end of their acquaintance.[18]

As he walked back to Grand Parade, Dr Beard replayed his conversation with Christiana. She protested his accusation so strongly that he briefly wondered if she really was telling the truth. He had heard many stories of food contamination before now and it was not unreasonable to consider the possibility that Christiana's sweets contained more than just chocolate. Food adulteration was a widespread practice in Victorian England, routinely carried out by manufacturers to keep production costs to a minimum. While some of the additives used were relatively harmless; bread was made from cheaper potato flour instead of wheat, for example, and milk was routinely diluted with water; others were not so innocuous. Poisonous copper sulphate provided the bright green colouring in jars of pickles and other preserved vegetables. Boric acid removed the sour taste from spoiled milk. Cheese was dyed with red lead and bread whitened with arsenic. Even a cup of tea could be harmful to health: retailers often reused old tea leaves by re-curling them and then adding colour with dangerous chemicals like copper.[19]

It wasn't only dietary staples, like bread and tea, which were affected by adulteration. Dangerous additives were commonplace in the confectionery industry and contemporaries were particularly concerned about its impact on children as the primary consumers of sweets and chocolates. One of the worst cases occurred in Bradford in 1858 when over 220 people, including a number of children, were accidentally poisoned with arsenic after buying peppermint lozenges from a market stall. Mr Neale, the manufacturer of these lozenges, used a recipe that called for 52 lbs of sugar but this was an expensive ingredient and he was keen to keep costs to a minimum. Instead, he substituted the sugar with calcium sulphate, a much cheaper white powder, but there was a mix-up at his suppliers and he received a cask of white powder that he mistakenly assumed was the calcium sulphate but was, in fact, arsenic trioxide. Having no knowledge of this mistake, Mr Neale prepared the lozenges as normal and transported them to Bradford market, completely unaware that each one contained a lethal dose of arsenic. Almost all of the peppermint lozenges were sold that day and a total twenty people lost their life, with a further 200 requiring hospital treatment.[20]

Although the poisoning of Mr Neale's confectionery was accidental, many confectioners routinely used hazardous substances without any consideration of the consequences. Less than one year after the Bradford poisoning, a group of children from a village in Devon became seriously ill and one almost died, after consuming sweets called bird's nests that had been coloured with lead. In a similar case at Bristol, one month later, a confectioner admitted to using a lead-based colouring to enhance the appearance of his products and causing six children to become seriously unwell. In an ironic twist, however, local authorities discovered that the confectioner had also become the victim of adulteration, after his supplier adulterated the colouring with arsenic.[21] Incidents like this led to the passing of the Adulteration of Food and Drink Act in 1860, the first legislative attempt to limit the use of dangerous additives and to establish better standards of food hygiene. As the act was not compulsory, it did not eradicate the practice of food adulteration but it did raise public awareness of this growing issue. In the meantime, many confectioners continued to adulterate sweets and chocolates with all manner of harmful substances.

Maynard's had been in business in Brighton since Dr Beard was a boy and he could not recall a single case of food poisoning in that time. It was, of course, entirely possible that John Maynard had started adulterating his cocoa powder with sawdust or his sugar with sulphate of lime, as many other confectioners did.[22] As a man of logic, however, Dr Beard could not accept that someone of Maynard's standing and reputation would risk it all on a single batch of poisonous chocolate creams. All the evidence pointed to Christiana, though she denied it again in January 1871 when Dr Beard confronted her for a second time. She desperately wished to renew their friendship but he refused and try as she might, Christiana could not convince him of her innocence. After this second meeting, Christiana called at Grand Parade with her mother and demanded that he retract his statement. While there was no 'absolute threat' of legal action made to Dr Beard, Christiana and Ann made it very clear that there would be consequences to his accusations. With no real evidence to substantiate his claims, he had little choice but to comply with her wish and retract his statement. He also destroyed around twenty of Christiana's letters which mentioned that fateful night in September.[23] In Dr Beard's mind, the incident in September had finally been laid to rest but this was only the beginning for Christiana. She was, of course, guilty of attempting to poison Emily Beard but what induced her to commit this crime has been hotly debated since that fateful night. It may have been a hereditary predisposition to madness or, more simply, an overwhelming feeling of malice towards the wife of the man she loved. Whether mad or bad, poisoning Emily and pleading her innocence to Dr Beard had thrilled Christina and she had demonstrated an almost-natural ability to seduce and deceive. How she obtained the poison and adulterated the chocolate cream remains a mystery but it had inspired an idea in Christiana of how to divert suspicion from herself and be redeemed by Dr Beard.

Chapter Five

"A Scattering of Death"

On a cold morning in March 1871, 13-year-old Benjamin Coultrop was selling newspapers in Spring Gardens when a lady approached him. She was wearing a thick veil over her face and enquired about Benjamin's employer. He told the lady that he had no employer and that he went out with the papers for himself each day. She appeared reassured by his answer and she purchased a paper before mentioning that she had bought herself a bag of chocolate creams and wondered if he might like them. Benjamin had never encountered such a generous customer before and he accepted her offer without hesitation, watching closely as she removed from her pocket a paper bag bearing the name 'Maynard's'. The lady then handed Benjamin the bag and left Spring Gardens as quickly as she had appeared.

Over the next few hours, Benjamin ate all but one of the chocolate creams. He gave the last one to his friend, Henry Diggins, who said it tasted funny and spat it out. Benjamin didn't notice any strange taste to his creams but he started to feel unwell about an hour after he finished the bag: his throat burned, he felt sick and his limbs were stiff. These symptoms did not improve over the next two days and his mother became so concerned that she took him to the hospital. He was admitted as an outpatient and treated for one week, after which he made a full recovery.

This wasn't the only strange incident to occur in March. A lady also visited a stationers on North Road and left on the counter a bag of chocolate creams bearing the name 'Maynard's'. The stationer's son, William Halliwell, saw the bag and ran after the lady but she was already out of sight by the time he reached the door. When the same lady returned to the shop a few days later, William offered her the bag of creams but she claimed they weren't hers and urged William to eat them. Over the course of the day, William ate around ten of the creams but became unwell later that evening. He felt hot, his legs ached and his whole body was stiff. It took six days for William to feel better and return to working in his father's shop. A few weeks later, he saw the lady leave another bag of Maynard's chocolate creams on the counter but he threw the bag on the fire, fearing a repeat of his previous illness.[1]

The lady responsible for these two incidents was Christiana Edmunds and they formed the first stage of her plan to be redeemed by Dr Beard. She had decided to frame the confectioner, John Maynard, for the poisoning of Emily Beard, while maintaining the façade that she was innocent of any wrongdoing. For Christiana, framing Maynard was not based on a personal vendetta; there was no real connection between the pair prior to 1870 and certainly not any enmity. He was simply the most logical candidate for such a crime because Emily Beard had no obvious enemies and the adulteration of confectionery was a well-known and well-established practice in this period. Part of what attracted Christiana to this plan was the ready availability of a wide range of poisons, of which arsenic was most popular and accounted for 45 per cent of deliberate poisonings between 1750 and 1914.[2] Arsenic was ideally suited to adulterating chocolate creams because it is tasteless, odourless and colourless, making it easy to hide in food or drink. It was also relatively cheap to buy, at only two pence per ounce during the nineteenth century.[3] But it did one have major drawback and this likely explains why Christiana did not use it in her plan to frame Maynard: by the mid-century, there were two tests for the forensic detection of arsenic and a number of skilled chemists capable of performing them. The first was invented by the chemist, James Marsh, who published his test in 1836. It involved heating a test sample with sulphuric acid and zinc to create a gas. This gas is then heated and confirms the presence of arsenic if it leaves behind any metallic deposits. While the Marsh test could detect minute amounts of arsenic, it was simplified in 1841 by the German chemist, Hugo Reinsch. This test is performed by dissolving the sample into a solution of hydrochloric acid and then inserting a strip of copper foil into it. If the strip turns black or dark grey, it indicates the presence of arsenic. Both the Marsh and Reinsch tests were immediately introduced into English courtrooms and were often used in combination in cases of criminal poisoning. Only one year before Christiana's attempt on Emily Beard's life for example, the Dudley poisoning case hit the national press. Fanny Oliver, a 28-year-old Milliner, was accused of murdering her husband by poisoning him with arsenic. The prosecution alleged that Fanny killed him because she wanted to re-establish a relationship with her former fiancé. At her trial in July 1869, Dr Hill, a Birmingham chemist, carried out the Reinsch test but found no traces of arsenic in the contents of Joseph's stomach. He extracted another sample and performed the Marsh test, finding this time one-hundredth of a grain of arsenic. Fanny was found guilty of murder and sentenced to death while the press and public argued over the reliability of chemical evidence.[4] What is most interesting about the Fanny Oliver case is that the Victorian thirst for murder trials had imparted a degree of understanding on the general public about the science of detection. This meant that ordinary people, like Christiana, knew about the Marsh and Reinsch tests and this perhaps accounts for her decision to spur arsenic, the nineteenth-century murderer's poison of choice, in favour of strychnine, a lesser-used but even deadlier weapon.

Strychnine was one of a number of poisons extracted from trees in the nineteenth century but it was, by far, the strongest, capable of killing an adult with a dose as low as 30mg, one-sixth of the required dosage for death by arsenic.[5] It is derived from the dried seeds of the Strychnos Nux-Vomica, a tree native to India, and was used widely in England from the 1820s. Despite being so lethal, strychnine's primary use was medicinal and it was prescribed for a wide range of ailments, from deafness and headache to rheumatism and cholera. One London-based physician, Dr R. Rowland, hailed strychnine as a wonder drug for women and used it to treat neuralgia, period pains, amenorrhoea and hysteria.[6] By the 1840s strychnine had also become a staple ingredient in pest control, particularly in the fight against rats, and was freely available for purchase by the general public.

Despite its wide availability and toxicity, deliberate poisoning by strychnine was relatively uncommon, accounting for only 41 of the 504 poisoning cases brought before the English courts between 1750 and 1914.[7] Even after the passing of the Pharmacy Act in 1868, which imposed stricter rules on its general purchase, there were more cases of poisoning by opium and prussic acid (cyanide) than strychnine.[8] Perhaps it was strychnine's bitter taste which made it less popular among Victorian would-be murderers. It was far more difficult to disguise the poison in food or drink, as demonstrated by the experience of Emily Beard and Henry Diggins, both of whom spat out the chocolate cream. While Benjamin Coultrop and William Halliwell noticed no strange taste, the sudden onset of symptoms illustrates the speed with which strychnine attacks the body. In fact, signs of strychnine poisoning can appear in as little as fifteen minutes and generally begin with a burning sensation in the throat, difficulty swallowing and a feeling of anxiety and restlessness. Because strychnine disrupts the nerve signals between the brain and the muscles, the victim next experiences painful contractions of the muscles throughout the body that gradually increase in strength and intensity. As the muscles become exhausted, the victim can no longer breathe and dies from asphyxiation. This process takes one to two hours and such a violent death leaves many victims in a state of opisthotonus, where the head, neck and spine are arched backwards, and rigor mortis quickly sets in. Fortunately, for Benjamin and William, there was not enough strychnine in the chocolate creams to kill them, though they experienced a number of unpleasant symptoms for several days after ingestion.

These early attempts then demonstrate that Christiana still had a way to go in her plan to frame Mr Maynard. There was no talk of any poisoning in town and no suspicion among the authorities, despite Benjamin Coultrop's admission to hospital. Perhaps his doctors believed he was suffering from tetanus, the only natural disease that resembles the effects of strychnine poisoning. Either way, neither Benjamin nor the hospital considered the possibility that he had been deliberately poisoned and so Christiana prepared to buy more of Maynard's chocolate creams and adulterate them with strychnine. While strychnine was readily available from any chemist, the passing of the Pharmacy Act in 1868 had regulated its sale to the general public. It could only be purchased, for example, if the buyer and seller were already acquainted, or were introduced through a witness who knew both parties. Once a sale was made, the seller had to label the poison with his name and address and enter the details of the transaction into a poison book before the buyer signed it to verify the transaction. By limiting access to dangerous poisons, it was hoped that the Pharmacy Act would discourage people from deliberate poisoning but there were, of course, ways around the legal technicalities, as Christiana would now prove.

On 28 March 1871, Christiana went to see Isaac Garrett, the chemist on Queen's Road who supplied her neuralgia medication. She bought some toilet articles and then asked Garrett if she could buy a 'small quantity of strychnine' because she and her husband were 'much annoyed' by some cats and wanted to get rid of them. Although Garrett had known Christiana as a customer for four years, he knew nothing personal about her, not even her name, and therefore had no notion that her story about the cats was untrue. He objected to her request on the grounds that strychnine was too strong a poison for destroying cats but Christiana assured him that 'no harm could possibly happen'. She said she had no children and that only she and her husband would handle the poison.[9] This pacified Garrett somewhat and he agreed to sell it to her if she brought a witness whom they both knew. After some consideration, Garrett suggested Caroline Stone, a milliner who lived three doors down, and instructed Christiana to go and fetch her.

Feeling uneasy, Christiana left Garrett's and covered her face with a veil before entering Caroline Stone's shop at 7 Queen's Road. Unsure of how to word her request, Christiana made small talk with Stone, purchased a lace veil and then left the shop. She waited outside for a few minutes before going in and asking Stone for a small favour. She introduced herself as Mrs Wood and explained that she and her husband were naturalists and wanted some poison for the purposes of stuffing a bird but Mr Garrett required a witness before he would sell it to her. Caroline Stone was taken aback by her customer's unusual request, having never heard anything like it in her thirty years in business. Despite her hesitation, the customer seemed very respectable and Stone had no reason to doubt her intentions so she agreed to accompany her to Mr Garrett's.

Back at number 10, Mr Garrett explained to Stone that the new Act had made it necessary to have the signature of a householder as a witness. She agreed to witness the transaction and watched as he placed ten grains of strychnine into a packet and then wrote the following in the poison book: 'March 28, 1871 – Mrs Wood, Hillside, Kingstown; Strychnia, 10 grains; destroying cats'. If Caroline Stone noticed that the entry contained no mention of stuffing birds, she kept quiet about it. She and Christiana signed the entry and then parted company, with Christiana confident that her true motives for the purchase remained a secret. With a fresh supply of strychnine, Christiana returned home to Gloucester Place and prepared for the second round of poisonings.

On a cold morning, just after Easter Monday in 1871, Christiana ventured again to Spring Gardens, the place where she had met Benjamin Coultrop at the beginning of March. Though only a mile from Gloucester Place, Spring Gardens was a very different

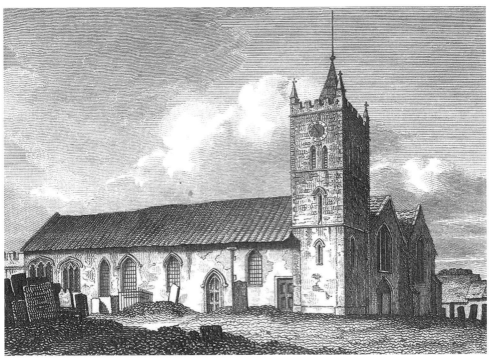

St John's Church in Margate was William Edmund's first commission and still stands today. (*Reproduced with kind permission of Anthony Lee*)

16 Hawley Square (far right) was Christiana's childhood home in Margate. (*Reproduced with kind permission of Raymond Godfrey*)

Sir William C. Ellis was an advocate of moral treatment and founded Southall Park Asylum in 1839. (*Wellcome Library, London*)

Christiana in the dock, sketched here with Dr Beard and his wife, Emily. (*Source unknown*)

Marine Terrace was the final home of Louisa Edmunds and the sad stage of her demise in 1867. (*Reproduced with kind permission of Anthony Lee*)

The seaside town of Brighton thrived in the nineteenth century and was one of the most fashionable resorts in the country. (*Creative Commons*)

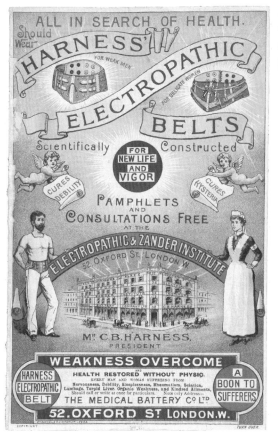

Electropathic belts were a popular way of treating nervous disorders, like hysteria, and were widely advertised in the popular press. (*Wellcome Library, London*)

Strychnine is a highly poisonous substance and is derived from the seeds of the Strychnos Nux-Vomica. (*Creative Commons*)

West Street was home to Maynard's confectionery shop and was the scene of Sidney Barker's murder in June 1871. (*Author's own collection*)

69 Grand Parade was the home of Elizabeth Boys, one of the recipients of the poisoned parcels. (*Creative Commons*)

John Humffreys Parry was a highly-respected Serjeant-at-Law and the man tasked with defending Christiana at her trial in 1872. (*Creative Commons*)

The prosecutor, William Ballantine, was sceptical of Christiana's insanity plea and believed she knew the difference between right and wrong. (*Creative Commons*)

Christiana was incarcerated here, at Newgate Prison, before facing trial at the Old Bailey in January 1872. (*Creative Commons*)

The interior of a typical cell in Newgate. (*Creative Commons*)

The exterior of Broadmoor, the country's first asylum for the criminally insane. (*Wellcome Library, London*)

Patients relax as part of their moral treatment at Broadmoor. (*Wellcome Library, London*)

neighbourhood to the one Christiana called home. An area of notorious poverty, its residents were blighted by some of the town's worst living conditions. When the Government Inspector, Edward Cresy, visited Brighton in 1849 to report on the town's sanitary condition, he had highlighted Spring Gardens and the surrounding streets as a major source of disease. Cresy observed that sulphurated hydrogen, arising from the excrement in nearby cesspools, was the source of sickness among its residents because 'this deadly poison pervades all the narrow breathing-places which are found at the backs of continued rows of buildings'. This problem was exacerbated by the poor quality of housing in the district:

> *Many of the houses are wretchedly damp, being constructed with inferior bricks and mortar made of sea sand. No methods are adopted for getting rid of even the pluvial waters, and the walls are covered with lichens; so that, added to the want of drainage, a constant decomposition of vegetable matter is going on.*[10]

While Brighton's dominance as a centre of tourism had brought great wealth to the town, much of this money was spent on improving leisure facilities and not on creating an infrastructure for its growing number of inhabitants. By 1860, for example, only one-quarter of Brighton's houses were drained into its eight miles of sewers while the remaining three-quarters relied on cesspools.[11] Commenting on this situation, William Kebbell, a local doctor, wrote that 'the streets and districts of the poor, both in filth and general untidiness, and the squalor of the inhabitants, are a disgrace to any civilised people'.[12]

In this place of poverty and disease, where Christiana could pass unrecognised, she soon met Emily Baker, the 9-year-old daughter of Jesse Baker, a painter, and his wife Harriett. She was playing alone outside when Christina approached her and struck up a conversation. She began by asking if Emily liked sweets before finding out her name, age and address. Once Christiana had this information, she handed Emily a bag of chocolate creams from Maynard's and watched as she excitedly ran home, blissfully unaware of the dangers inside. Christiana returned to Spring Gardens a few days later, in a bold move which brought her dangerously close to being detected, and called at Emily's house. Her mother, Harriett, opened the door, and Christiana asked her if any children in the area had recently been taken ill. Harriett assumed that the lady at her door was a district visitor, a person who visited poorer families on behalf of the Church of England, and recounted how her daughter had vomited for three days after eating some chocolates. Harriett said she was keen to find the lady who gave them to Emily, prompting Christiana to make her excuses and return to Gloucester Place. Had Emily been at home that day and recognised Christiana, the course of her life would have been very different. But this experience unnerved Christiana nonetheless and, from now on, she adopted a new practice that involved hiring a young boy to go to Maynard's and purchase chocolate creams on her behalf. One such boy was 12-year-old, William Tye, who Christiana met on North Street in April. She asked him to fetch three ounces of chocolate creams and gave him one shilling to cover the cost. When William returned from Maynard's, Christiana took the bag of chocolate creams and switched it for a bag hidden in her pocket. These were the creams that she had poisoned at home and Christina distracted him to ensure that he did not see her make the switch and realise the ruse. Now all she had to do was tell the boy that he had purchased the wrong creams and get him to exchange them at Maynard's for a different type,[13] to ensure that her poisoned creams were distributed randomly to other customers and to guarantee a fresh supply for adulteration. Even more advantageous was the sense of anonymity it brought to Christiana; nobody would suspect her of foul play if she was not in Maynard's shop at the time of purchase.

Christiana did, however, return to Maynard's shop one last time but not to buy his chocolate creams. She went to make a complaint, the first one John Maynard had received in his twenty-eight years as a confectioner in Brighton. He was taken aback when she told him that she and a friend had been unwell after eating some of his chocolate creams in September. He was even more upset to hear that she had bought another bag in March, which had tasted very unpleasant and made her throat burn. Being entirely innocent of adulteration, Maynard could hardly accept responsibility for Christiana's illness but he took her complaint seriously and tasted some of the creams for himself. He found nothing wrong with their taste but consented to her suggestion that the creams be chemically analysed. From Maynard's, Christiana headed to see Julius Schweitzer, a chemist at 86 King's Road, and requested that he perform the analysis. She told him the same story about the poisoning in September but Schweitzer treated the matter very lightly at first, believing Christiana to be 'nervous and fanciful'. But Christiana had brought him a sample of her adulterated creams and, as soon as he had tasted one, he quickly changed his mind and agreed to conduct the analysis. At this, Christiana left Schweitzer's, confident that her ruse to frame John Maynard would now have all the credibility it needed and that she would be exonerated finally for the poisoning of Emily Beard.

In the meantime, Christiana focused her attention on maintaining a steady supply of strychnine by cultivating a relationship with Isaac Garrett. She visited his shop frequently, talked with him at length about her garden and twice brought him a bundle of home-grown asparagus, all while maintaining the façade that she was Mrs Wood of Hillside. On 15 April she told Garrett that that cats were 'as destructive as ever' and that she needed more strychnine to kill them. Garrett was again hesitant to dispense strychnine for this purpose and requested that she fetch Caroline Stone. At her shop, Christiana purchased another veil, prompting Caroline Stone to agree to witness the transaction and Garrett dispensed another ten grains of strychnine. Christiana now had in her possession enough strychnine to kill twenty adults or at least twice as many children.[14] At the beginning of May, she returned to Garrett's to purchase strychnine for the third time. She told the chemist that she and her husband had decided to leave Brighton and move to 'Devonshire' but first she needed a little strychnine for the purposes of killing a dog who was too old and sick to accompany them. Garrett cautioned her again about using a poison as strong as strychnine but he supplied her with another ten grains, this time without a witness.

Christiana's story about wanting to kill a dog was not a complete fabrication. There was a dog at her house but it was not old and diseased as she had led Garrett to believe. It was, in fact, the favourite dog of Louisa Taylor, a fellow lodger at 16 Gloucester Place where Christiana had lived since 27 March, having moved with her mother from the house next door. On 27 May, the house servant, Charlotte Pettit noticed Christiana playing with the dog on the upstairs landing. Half an hour later, Christiana had disappeared but the dog had become unwell and began to twist and writhe, as if in agony. The dog died shortly after and Miss Taylor sent for Henry Swayster, the son of a bird stuffer, who delivered it to a local taxidermist, Robert Bragnor. When Bragnor opened the box and saw the dog, he knew instantly that it had been poisoned because of its 'peculiar rigidity' and 'inward bending' of the backbone. The dog's mouth was also of an 'offensive character', curled into that devilish grin known as Resus Sardonicus, another indicator of poisoning by strychnine. Of all the animals he had stuffed over the years, Bragnor later said that he had never seen one in such a state.[15] This sad incident aroused much suspicion among the taxidermist and the lodgers of 17 Gloucester Place but nobody truly believed that Christiana Edmunds, a well-educated and well-bred lady, might be capable of a crime like poisoning. Her social background had afforded her all the protection she needed to continue poisoning Brighton's unsuspecting public over the summer of 1871.

Chapter Six

"For the Pure Love of Deception"

Early on the morning of Monday 12 June, Charles Miller was on his way back to his lodgings on West Street after going for a walk around town. This was Miller's second day on holiday in Brighton, having travelled by train from London on Saturday with his brother, sister and her family. As he strolled down West Street he called in at Maynard's sweet shop and asked the assistant, Annie Meadows, for a bag of her best chocolate creams. Maynard's stocked three types of chocolate creams but the best, by far, were the French variety which were kept in the bottom compartment of a glass case on the counter. The demand for these creams had been very high lately; Annie and her fellow assistants had served a number of young boys over the last few weeks but, rather unusually, every bag of creams had been returned and exchanged for another. As nobody had reported a problem with their taste or quality, these creams were put back into the glass case on the counter and then placed into a bag by Annie and handed over to Charles Miller.[1]

When Miller returned to his lodgings at 30 West Street, he was warmly welcomed by his 4-year-old nephew, Sidney, to whom he gave the first chocolate cream from the bag. He then handed a cream to his brother, Ernest, before eating a few himself. But not long after, Miller noticed a strange, coppery taste in his throat and his legs felt heavy and stiff. He tried to get up from his chair but fell backwards and a second attempt left him feeling as though his body was 'without joints'.[2] Charles was so unwell that the landlady, Mrs Freeman, sent for James Tuke, a surgeon who lived close by. After a full examination,

Tuke could find no obvious cause for Miller's strange symptoms but he was certain that the chocolate creams were not responsible and declared them perfectly safe to consume. A few hours later, Miller began to feel much better and, at 4.00 pm, he gave another chocolate cream to his nephew, Sidney.[3]

But within minutes of eating the cream, Sidney suddenly began to cry and called to his uncle that he didn't like the chocolate. His mother, Selicia, ran to him and picked him up. She asked him what was the matter but Sidney was unable to answer her because his muscles had already started to spasm. The family called again for a doctor and a nearby surgeon, Richard Rugg, arrived soon after to find Sidney 'in strong convulsions'.[4] The family quickly told Rugg about the chocolate creams and how the boy's uncle had fallen ill earlier that day. Recognising this as the work of poison, Rugg applied to the nearest chemist for an emetic and, in the meantime, placed a mixture of cold water and vinegar to Sidney's head in an attempt to control his increasingly violent convulsions. Sadly, before the emetic arrived, Sidney suffered one final convulsion and died in the doctor's arms.

Had the first doctor, James Tuke, attended Sidney Barker, the aftermath of his tragic death could have played out very differently. Richard Rugg, on the other hand, knew that Sidney had been poisoned and was keen to know how this little boy had met his end. In cases of a suspicious death, it was the doctor's duty to inform the authorities and Rugg duly contacted the police and the coroner after he left the grieving family at West Street. In the meantime, Sidney's uncle, Ernest, went to Maynard's to purchase some more chocolate creams and handed them over to William Gibbs, the police inspector in charge of the investigation.

In his twenty years on the Brighton Police Force, William Gibbs had become accustomed to dealing with drunks, thieves and prostitutes but he had relatively little experience with poisoners. In 1863, while Gibbs was still a constable, Mary Ann Day, a mother of eight from

Kemptown, died after eating a mince pie laced with arsenic. The police arrested Mary's fiancé, William Sturt, and alleged that he had poisoned her after changing his mind about their impending marriage. William was tried in March 1863 but the jury found him not guilty and her case remained unsolved. A few years later, after Gibbs' promotion to sergeant, Doctor Alfred Warder was accused of murdering his wife, Ellen, by administering doses of aconite, or wolf's bane, to her over the course of a month. Before Warder could be arrested and tried, he fled to London and committed suicide by drinking cyanide. It later transpired that Warder's first two wives had died of unnatural causes but it was, by then, too late for an investigation to be made into the doctor's marital history.

While Inspector Gibbs shared Rugg's suspicions towards the chocolate creams purchased at Maynard's, he could not be certain that a crime had been committed until he saw the results of the post-mortem, the next stage in the process of investigating a suspicious death. This was carried out the next day by Richard Rugg who found Sidney's body to be 'unusually rigid' but otherwise in a very healthy condition. The only organ in which Rugg could find any damage was the brain; it appeared 'slightly congested' but this was, he claimed, to be expected in a case of death by convulsions. [5] Overall, there was nothing to indicate the cause of Sidney's death and the borough coroner, David Black, requested that he remove Sidney's stomach to allow for further investigation by an expert. Rugg duly carried out his request and placed the stomach and its contents into a glass jar which he then handed over to Inspector Gibbs.

By 1871, it had become standard practice for coroners to consult with a chemical expert in cases of an unexplained death, especially where poisoning was suspected. While local doctors, like Richard Rugg, were capable of and responsible for carrying out post-mortems, they often lacked the required specialist knowledge to detect and identify poison. Rugg, for example, would later admit that the Barker case was the first time he had ever seen a case of strychnine poisoning and he therefore had no idea how to diagnosis or detect this poison in the human body. The cost of consulting with an expert could be high but it was a necessary expense in the process of determining the cause of death. For the analysis, David Black hired Dr Henry Letheby, a chemical analyst and public health official from London, who had risen to become one of the country's leading medical experts. In fact, Dr Letheby acted as a medical witness in twelve criminal poisoning cases during his career, a figure which ranked him the fourth most-consulted expert of the nineteenth century.[6]

On the evening of 16 June, Inspector Gibbs travelled to London to personally deliver the glass jar containing Sidney's stomach and two packets of Mr Maynard's chocolate creams to Dr Letheby. The packet marked '1' contained the creams purchased by Ernest Miller on the day that Sidney died while the second packet, marked '2', was bought on 15 June by Charles Miller and Inspector Gibbs. While Gibbs returned to Brighton, Dr Letheby set to work straightaway by examining the contents of the glass jar. Like Rugg, he found Sidney's stomach to be in a very healthy condition and its contents smelled faintly of chocolate. He looked for signs of irritation, which would indicate poisoning by arsenic or antimony, but found nothing. Having heard the violent circumstances of Sidney's death, he next considered a mineral poison, like strychnine, or its close relative, brucine,[7] and extracted a sample from Sidney's stomach for testing. Dr Letheby performed the colour test, a method reliably used for the last decade to detect the presence of mineral poisons, which was quick and simple to carry out. He began by mixing the test sample with a little sulphuric acid and some potassium dichromate. This produced a vivid purple colour and he then waited for the sample to change colour. If it turned red, it indicated the presence of strychnine and, sure enough, the sample turned to red only a few minutes later. To be certain of the result, Letheby performed another, though slightly different, version of the colour reaction test. He extracted another sample from Sidney's stomach but, this time, mixed it with ferric chloride. Within seconds, the sample turned to blue, proving beyond all doubt that Sidney Barker was a victim of deliberate poisoning by strychnine.[8]

Back in Brighton, the news of Sidney Barker's death began to spread around the town while Christiana's poisoning spree continued unabated. Only a few days after his death, Christiana visited Cole's grocery shop on Church Street and purchased a few small articles. She was served by the owner's wife, Harriett Cole, who knew her as a regular customer. In a scene reminiscent of the poisoning of William Halliwell, Christiana dropped a paper bag in a zinc pail by the door and left the shop, knowing that Harriett would find it but hoping that she wouldn't realise who had left it there. Later in the day, when Harriett retrieved the bag, she opened it up to find several large and small chocolate creams and three lemon bull's-eyes inside. Harriett ate two of the bulls-eyes and gave the other to her daughter who complained of a funny taste and spat it out. The chocolate creams were given the next day to one of Harriett's customers, 10-year-old Henry Walker, who took them home as a gift to his mother, Caroline. She ate a piece of the larger chocolate cream and was not prepared for what happened next:

In about ten minutes after eating it I had a very strange sensation in my head. I felt as if my eyes were coming out; something seemed to strain them. I then got up and tried to get a glass of water. I got the water but could not put it to my mouth because my hands and arms shook. I then felt that I was losing the use of my limbs altogether. With a great effort I got upstairs and fell down on a chair in the parlour. I was quite alone in the house ... not able to reach the front or back door to call anyone.[9]

It was forty-five minutes before Henry returned to the house and could fetch help for his mother. Like many of Christiana's other victims,

Caroline was fortunate enough to make a full recovery without medical intervention but did not report the incident to the police nor to John Maynard. Christiana had not yet done enough to arouse suspicion of wholesale poisoning but, when she received a notice to attend Sidney Barker's inquest, it appeared that her efforts had finally paid off. The police had heard about her analysis at Schweitzer's and had cited her to give evidence against John Maynard. Christiana rushed to Grand Parade to inform Dr Beard, in the hope that he might finally believe her story about the attempt on Emily. But Dr Beard was working away and his wife did not want to inform him of the inquest by letter, much to Christiana's distress. Nevertheless, appearing at the inquest was an opportunity she relished because it gave her the chance to play the innocent victim, to encourage popular hatred of John Maynard and, more importantly, to be noticed again by Dr Beard.

In the nineteenth century, it was usual practice to hold an inquest within a few days of a suspicious death. This involved the coroner calling on between twelve and twenty-four men of good repute to act as jurors and to appear at the specified time and place. Brighton's coroner, David Black, had postponed Sidney Barker's inquest pending the results of Dr Letheby's investigation but, once he had them, he called on his jury to assemble on the afternoon of Thursday, 22 June. Victorian inquests were held in the pub and David Black liked to use one close to his home and office at 58 Ship Street. Like the majority of coroners in this period, Black was a lawyer by trade and a partner in the law firm, Black and Freeman. He was appointed Brighton's first coroner on 1 January 1855 and had some experience of poisoning cases, having directed the inquests of Mary Ann Day in 1863 and Dr Alfred Warder's wife, Ellen, three years later, but he had never seen a case which had resulted in such a violent death for a little boy.

The inquest into the death of Sidney Barker opened like any other: the jury had the opportunity to view his body before hearing the evidence of witnesses with relevant information, like Christiana, or who were present at the death. Charles Miller, Sidney's uncle, and Richard Rugg retold the events of that fateful day before Dr Letheby gave the much-anticipated results of his chemical analysis. He explained that he had found a quarter of a grain of strychnine inside Sidney's stomach and this was more than enough to kill a small child. He had also analysed for traces of poison some of the individual chocolate creams which were delivered to him by Inspector Gibbs. He found the red, pink and brown ones were perfectly safe to consume but the white creams had tested positive for strychnine. At this point, David Black interjected and informed the jury that strychnine was used extensively in the preparation of vermin killers. It was a poison with a distinctive bitter taste which made it unsuitable in the colouring or flavouring of confectionery. If strychnine was not part of the manufacturing process, said the coroner, it followed that Sidney Barker had been deliberately poisoned. But before the jury retired to discuss a verdict, David Black called Christiana Edmunds, one of John Maynard's alleged victims.

This was the opportunity that Christiana had been waiting for and she intended to make the most of her testimony. In her dramatic fabrication, she described in detail the events which took place in the previous September, without any reference to Emily Beard. She instead talked of the 'violent internal pains' that she experienced after eating one of Maynard's chocolate creams – and again in March when she bought another bag. This time, she felt even worse: 'I was seized as before, but more violently and in a slightly different way. There was the same burning in the throat, and a feeling of lightness in that region. The saliva kept flowing into the mouth and I was seized with a trembling all over and felt an indescribable sensation'. Only a glass of brandy and water and some castor oil, she told the jury, could relieve her of this incredible suffering. Christiana's testimony had the jury gripped and she was now ready to deliver the final blow to John

Maynard's reputation as she described the occasion on which she made her complaint:

> *On the same day I took the remainder of the chocolate creams to Mr Maynard and told him of what had occurred. He assured me that I was mistaken in supposing that it was the chocolate creams which had affected me ... Some more were brought and tasted but they seemed all right. Mrs Maynard also tasted one of the creams I had originally bought and found that there was nothing the matter with it. Mr Maynard told me he was much obliged to me for coming and he would communicate with his French agents. He also said he should be willing for me to have any analysis made that I desired. As I did not feel satisfied I went straight from Mr Maynard's to Mr Schweitzer's.*

At this point, John Penfold, the solicitor appearing on behalf of John Maynard, asked Christiana why she did not present the results of Schweitzer's analysis to his client. She said there seemed no point because Maynard had been sceptical and prejudiced towards herself and her complaint.

Interestingly, Schweitzer's analysis did not reveal the presence of strychnine. Perhaps he lacked the necessary skill to uncover Christiana's poison, or perhaps she deliberately gave him a batch of unadulterated chocolate creams. If Maynard was found to be in possession of strychnine-laced confectionery then her poisoning spree would be over long before her much-anticipated reunion with Dr Beard. Schweitzer's analysis, however, did find something unusual:

> *The cream cocoa consists of small, irregular round cakes, filled with a soft, white sugar composition. After examination, it was found that this white composition of some of these cakes, or balls, had a distinct*

metallic taste, whilst others were perfectly free from it ... The metal
with which the so-called cream ... is impregnated is, in fact, zinc.

While zinc can be hazardous to human health in large doses it was commonly used by confectioners to add colour to sweets and chocolate. Schweitzer's analysis, then, had done little to convince the jury of Maynard's guilt. When questioned, the confectioner could not account for the presence of strychnine in his stock. He told the jury that he did not keep any poison on his premises because his pet cat took care of any vermin. Since February, he obtained all of his French stock, including the creams that killed Sidney Barker, from a confectionery wholesaler in London and had conducted a thorough investigation after Christiana complained to him. Two of his assistants, Kate Page and Annie Meadows, testified to this fact and neither could think of a way in which strychnine might have found its way into his shop.

If the shop was not the source of contamination then it was not unreasonable to suggest that strychnine had entered the chocolate creams at the point of manufacture. The coroner now called George Ware, the wholesaler from whom John Maynard bought his stock. He had travelled from London for the inquest and had been in business there since 1839. He claimed that this was the first complaint he had received about the creams and did not keep any poisons in his factory. When it came to making the chocolate creams, he used only sugar and cream of tartar to make the filling, some vanilla for flavouring and a dye called cochineal, made from the dried body of an insect. Ware admitted, however, that the factory did have a problem with vermin and that he hired exterminators to kill them and his team of exterminators used dogs, traps and poison but he could not say for certain if this contained any strychnine.

David Black was now out of ideas. If the poison did not originate at the point of manufacture nor the point of sale, he could not understand how Sidney Barker might have ingested it. In summing up, he said to the jury that the 'most reasonable hypothesis' was that it happened through some 'misadventure' at Ware's factory but a charge of criminal negligence did not seem appropriate for a man who had operated without complaint for over three decades. As for John Maynard, Black believed that he had taken every 'reasonable precaution' after Christina made her complaint but it was unfortunate that she did not communicate to him the results of her analysis. Black thus recommended that the jury follow the medical evidence and declare that Sidney Barker had died as a result of strychnine poisoning but acknowledge that how he came to ingest it remained a mystery. When the jury later returned their verdict, they agreed completely with David Black but made one recommendation to George Ware: that better care be taken when using vermin poison at his factory.[10]

For John Maynard, the verdict came as a great relief. The jury had found him innocent of any wrongdoing, though he volunteered to destroy his supply of French stock to ensure the prevention of another tragedy. Christiana's campaign to slur his reputation had failed and, had she ceased her poisoning campaign after the inquest, her crimes would have gone undetected in history. But the thrill of the chase was too enticing and she was not hampered by feelings of remorse towards Sidney Barker. In fact, his death had given her another reason to communicate with Dr Beard and she penned the following letter in the days after the inquest:

Caro Mio, I have been so miserable since my last letter to you. I can't go on without ever speaking to you. What made me write so? I thought, perhaps, it would be better for both of us, but I have not strength of mind to bear it. We met La Sposa [wife] *the day after her return, and were glad to see her back again. La Madre* [mother] *thought she looked very thin and careworn; I hope she will feel the good now from her change. You must have missed her. I didn't enter on the poisoning case on the street, but I called and told her that I was obliged to appear at the inquest in a few days, and I hoped she would send you a paper and let you know; but she said 'No, she did not wish to unsettle you'. However, dear, I mean you to know about this dreadful poisoning case, especially as I had to give evidence; and I know how interested you would be in it, as you told me you would give anything to know what La Sposa swallowed. I sent you the analysis and have no means of knowing if it was sent you. Yes, through my analysis, the police found me out, and cited me to appear. You can fancy what I felt; such an array of gentlemen; and that clever Dr Letheby, looking so ugly and so terrific frightened me more than anyone else; for, if I gave wrong symptoms, of course he would have known. You fancy my feelings, standing therefore before the public, looking very rosy and frightened as I was. When I saw the reporters' pens going and taking down all I uttered, Burns' lines rushed to my memory: 'the chield amang them taking notes, and faith he'll prent it'.*

Christiana's reference to Robert Burns is from the poem, *On the Late Captain Groses's Peregrinations Thro' Scotland*, which was published in 1789. By mentioning these lines, she was doing more than just displaying her literary knowledge; she echoed Burns' famous warning to be wary of her words, for any fault or flaw in her testimony would not pass unnoticed. We have to wonder if Dr Beard understood her cryptic message or simply interpreted her reference as a fear of standing before the jury. Her letter continued:

I did the best I could, thankful when I had finished. It seemed so long and my evidence [Blank here]. As the jury had nothing to say, my heart was thankful. When Mr Gell and Penfold attacked me – Mr G.: 'Why didn't I show Maynard the analysis?' – it was so sudden, my ideas all left me, and I merely said because I found Mr Maynard so sceptical and prejudiced, and I thought I had done sufficient. Oh! Why didn't I say as I meant 'Because I supposed Mr M. would take the same steps as I had done, or else destroyed his stock, and that, if those sold to Mr Miller were from the same stock, I had warned him against these, – he was answerable'. If I had only said that – for I had no friendly feeling toward Mr M. – that man's chocolates had been the cause of great suffering to me. The Inspector said he wished I had spoken as I felt and as I did to him when came to me, earnestly and energetically. But La Madre told me I should be thought flippant: so you see I was subdued ... You see there were two poisons. Zinc was in La Sposa's and mine. I was troubled to describe the taste. The reporters smiled when I said castor oil and brandy. The coroner said, 'Ah! Your usual remedy'. I was stupid. He is so deaf. I was told to stand close to him. I took care to turn my back on the jury all I could. They were all very polite to me, even that fierce Mr Penfold. Dr Letheby's evidence was so interesting, and showed the different sweets in one glass tube, yet separated. His physique is large and grand, like his mind. Now, darling, rest assured, through the whole affair, I have never mentioned your name or La Sposa's, and if I had been asked to mention a friend, I should say Mrs Dix. She is very kind and fond of me, and would have come forward had they wanted her to help me. No; the rack shouldn't have torn your name from me; and the only reason I said September was, that you might see I had concealed nothing.

Christiana here implies that she omitted Emily Beard's name from the inquest in an effort to save the Beards' involvement in such a tragic and scandalous case. But in reality, she could never mention Emily because, if questioned by the coroner, her version of events would point the finger of suspicion firmly in Christiana's direction. Christiana cleverly disguises her deceit in exaggerated terms of affection which make her letter read like a conversation between lovesick teenagers. Her desperate plea for vindication continues in the closing paragraph:

My dear boy, do esteem me now. I am sure you must. What a trial it was to go through, that inquest! La Madre was angry I ever had the analysis; but you know why I had it – to clear myself in my dear friend's eyes. She always says nothing was meant by you. No, darling; you wanted an excuse for my being so slighted. I never think of it; it was all a mistake. I called on La Sposa and told her how I got on. She said my evidence was very nice. She didn't ask me to come; but perhaps she mustn't. Now there is no reason. La Madre says if you were at home she is sure you would ask me just the same as ever.

Come and see us, darling; you have time now. La Madre and I have been looking forward to your holiday to see you. She wants to know how you get on and how you like the North. Don't be biased by any relatives; act as your kind heart tells you, and make a poor little thing happy, and fancy a long, long, bacio [kiss] *from*
DOROTHEA.

Christiana's reinvention as Dorothea is all part of her plan to deceive Dr Beard and portray herself as the innocent victim of John Maynard's adulteration. She was perhaps inspired by Saint Dorothea, a fourth-century woman who was tried and tortured for her Christian beliefs. On the way to her execution, Dorothea met a lawyer called Theophilus who mockingly asked her to send fruits from God's garden when she arrived there. When Theophilus later received a basket of fruit and flowers, he realised that Dorothea was telling the truth and he converted to Christianity. In this imagination of events, then, Christiana was a tortured woman, waiting desperately for Dr Beard to believe her so that a reunion might take place. But there was to be no reconciliation nor a long, long 'bacio'. Christiana's appearance at the inquest did nothing to change Dr Beard's opinion of her: he did not rush to Gloucester Place to see her on his return from the North nor did he respond to her letter. In Christiana's mind, her only option was to step up her campaign and destroy John Maynard, once and for all.

Chapter Seven

"Who Knows Where This May End"

On the afternoon on 27 June, Sidney Barker's father, Albert, received the following anonymous letter:

Sussex Square, June 27, 1871.

Sir, – Having seen the result of the investigation of the inquest Thursday last, I feel great surprise to find that no blame is attached to anyone. I have felt great interest in the case, and fully sympathise in your sad loss. Great dissatisfaction is felt at the result by most of the inhabitants, and we all feel it rests with yourself now to take proceedings against Mr Maynard. As a parent myself I could not rest satisfied, nor would one in a hundred. I trust you will come forward for your own sake and the public good. You shall have all the assistance possible. I feel sure the young lady will willingly come forward, as I know, from good authority, she was very dissatisfied with Maynard's conduct; of course suppose he would have taken the same step she did and have them analysed. I can only say that Mr Maynard, after being duly warned that his chocolates were injurious, and had made three persons ill, ought to have them analysed or destroy them. The public mind is not satisfied; and feel great blame is attached to him for selling to your family chocolates from the same stocks he had been warned against. He spoke of investigating, and what was in his investigating? Merely looking over and tasting a few chocolates with his shopwoman. Why, the young lady, was not satisfied with that, even; and, as to writing to his French agent, it appears he never did. I hope no monetary considerations will prevent you from taking proceedings. The Brighton inhabitants are all up in arms at the laxity of proceedings in the want of justice, and will assist you in every way, and, with the facts tried before unbiased and unprejudiced men, I think Mr Maynard will not escape scot free. My feeling of disgust is felt by most of the influential and respectable inhabitants of this town.

I am, Sir,

An Old Inhabitant And Seeker of Justice

P.S. The Town Council cannot take up the case again; it rests with you, and you shall receive all the aid we can offer. The papers are taking this up, both Brighton and London. See the London Observer.

This mysterious letter was followed the next day by another:

Vernon Terrace, June 28, 1871

Sir – I hear there is a general feeling of indignation at the termination of the proceedings of the inquest of Thursday last; that a jury should be so lenient, and attach no blame to anyone, is unheard of. All that can be done now is for you to make further investigations, and it certainly seems a duty to yourself and the public, who will, I am assured, never let the matter rest. Why is Mr Maynard to be screened, and the whole affair glossed over? He was warned of his sweets, and yet he deliberately sells some of the very same to your family, and you are lose your poor child through his great negligence. Why didn't he investigate or destroy his sweets at once? Are people's complaints to be disregarded because he excuses himself by saying the witnesses' versions are fanciful? Why didn't he see her friend? I say he took no means to ascertain what was wrong, and is certainly answerable for selling those sweets after being warned. Your lawyer (excuse me for saying it) did very little on your behalf. He never taxed Mr Maynard with not taking steps to know what the sweets really contained, and for daring to sell them without a proper investigation, never even waiting to inquire of the French agent he had them from. Of course you cannot rest supine; no one could sustain the loss you have done and rest satisfied. There is a report current that you are going to take proceedings against Maynard. We all hope to hear, if you do not, someone will take the matter up, and you may feel certain when the case is tried before the intelligent men, you may get redress for the wrongs you have received. In our local paper of yesterday, there is a paragraph saying 'what a strange verdict,' and you cannot of course rest satisfied with. Such a deadly poison as strychnine ought hardly to be in existence. I believe other evidence might be brought forward, having heard of several who have been made ill by Maynard's sweets. I have no doubt that you will take some further steps. No parent could let the loss of his child be passed over in this cursory way. The Brighton public earnestly hope you will do something, for who knows where this may end? More of these sweets may be sold by the maker, and other lives lost. The greatest sympathy is felt for yourself and family; and in saying what I have, I have only expressed the feelings of most of the Brighton inhabitants.

I remain yours truly,

G.C.B.

The author of these anonymous letters was, of course, Christiana. She had decided to appeal directly to the family of Albert Baker in her attempt to frame John Maynard for the death of their son. It is interesting to note her sympathetic sentiments towards the grieving family and we have to wonder if they were an expression of genuine remorse. Her slander towards John Maynard, however, make it more reasonable to suggest that she used the family's grief as a means of manipulating them into action. Her letters are increasingly assertive in tone, yet smack of her desperation. She penned a third letter two days later:

Brighton, July 1 1871

Dear Sir – Having seen your letter in the Daily News,[1] permit me to say that, as you seem doubtful as to whom you are to proceed against, it is generally thought that the seller of the chocolate is the proper person, and it is the firm conviction, with all who know the case that this man, after being warned, and making no investigation, is certainly answerable. Had he taken common precautions – had his sweets properly examined – this sad event might never have occurred. Are persons' warnings to be disregarded because he chooses to think them nervously fanciful? Such negligence ought not to be tolerated. A letter from Mr Ware's solicitor makes the case worse, for he says if the sweetmeats were supplied by him, the poison must have got into them after leaving the premises. Now you have good grounds for pursuing your investigations, for who supplied these chocolates to the seller? As the Brighton Times observed to-day, the case cannot be dropped; that you are the person to take proceedings, and of course cannot rest satisfied – the public will not, I frankly confess. Had I lost my child in such a sad way, as a parent I should feel myself in duty bound to take proceedings against the seller of the sweets. Justice I would have, and you have certainly not had it shown in your case. Excuse the liberty I take in advising you, but you may not read the papers, and know what it hoped for and expected from you.

I am, Sir, respectfully yours,
A London Tradesman Now A Visitor At Brighton

P.S. I am sure that many London tradesmen, with myself, will second you in your efforts.[2]

Christiana had now exhausted every possible method of persuading Albert to take action against Mr Maynard. She had talked of his parental responsibilities, of public safety, outrage among the press, a general need for justice and had even identified herself as a London tradesman, in an attempt to portray unity with Albert, a humble, dressing-case maker from Clapham. But, for Albert, her letters had become a growing nuisance and he handed them over to the Metropolitan Police who, it appears, took no further action on the matter.

Back in Brighton, Christiana's attention was temporarily diverted from John Maynard by an unexpected visit from Dr Beard. This was the first time she had seen him in six months and, like the last time, it was her deepest hope that he might renew their friendship. But Dr Beard intended this meeting to be their last. He could suffer her bombardment of letters no longer and told her 'this correspondence must cease; it is not good for either of us'.[3] Her reaction was surprisingly positive, prompting the doctor to confess that he had shown all of her letters to his wife, Emily. Christiana was completely stunned by this revelation and could not understand why Dr Beard would show such intimate correspondence to an outside party. In her mind, Emily's knowledge accounted for Dr Beard's coolness towards her and the decline of their friendship but, when asked, he claimed he had not 'respected her so much' since the attempt on his wife in September 1870. After he left Gloucester Place, Ann found Christiana pacing the room and saying 'I shall go mad! I shall go mad!' Ann tried to calm her daughter down but her efforts were in vain. She warned her instead of the dangers of becoming a slave to her passions: 'You are mad already', she told Christiana, 'you of all people, ought to be particular'. Ann was, of course, referring to the family history of insanity[4] but this reminder was not enough to pacify her daughter's mind or make her realise that her fairy tale romance with Dr Beard would never end in the manner she most desired.

As Christiana's mental state further deteriorated, her poisoning scheme became increasingly complex and her web of deceit even more intricate. The first casualty was Mrs Wood of Hillside, the alter ego she had created to falsely procure strychnine from Isaac Garrett, who was dropped in favour of a new and more ingenious method. By 8 June she was ready to test it out and had a boy deliver the following note to Garrett's:

Messrs Glaisyer and Kemp will be much obliged if Mr Garrett could supply them with a little strychnia. They are in immediate want of half an ounce, or if not able, a smaller quantity will do. Will Mr Garrett send it in a bottle, and sealed up? The bearer can be safely trusted with it.

Glaisyer and Kemp, 11 and 12 North Street.

John Kemp and Thomas Glaisyer were chemists and business partners with a well-established shop in the centre of Brighton. Christiana's reinvention as Glaisyer and Kemp was a clever move because she knew that they were well-acquainted with Isaac Garrett and that chemists frequently supplied each other with drugs in times of a shortage. There were only two factors that she had not considered: firstly, that Isaac Garrett only had a drachm, the equivalent to one-eighth of an ounce and, secondly, that he required an order note before he could confirm the purchase. He wrote these requirements in a short letter that was handed to the same errand boy and delivered directly to Christiana. She then penned the following response:

Messrs Glaisyer and Kemp will be quite satisfied with a drachm of strychnia till their own arrives, and thank Mr Garrett for supplying them. Their signature always being sufficient before in their business transactions. Should Mr Garrett feel the least hesitation in supplying them, they must apply elsewhere.

Glaisyer and Kemp, 11 and 12 North Street.

On receipt of this letter, Isaac Garrett was convinced of the order's authenticity and he placed the drachm of strychnine into a bottle which he labelled with his name and address, in accordance with current legislation. He took two shillings and sixpence from the boy and handed him the poison with one shilling and three pence in change; a small sum for such a deadly substance. Christiana's plan had worked perfectly and, back at Gloucester Place, she used this measure of strychnine to adulterate a fresh batch of Maynard's creams. Christiana then paid a boy to return these creams to Maynard's shop where the assistants would unwittingly pass them on to unsuspecting customers. This was how Sidney Barker had met his tragic end and how Christiana had cleverly avoided detection. Had Christiana returned these in person, she would have been identified as a witness, if not as a suspect, and her poisoning spree brought to an abrupt end. But Christiana had no intention of stopping and it was, perhaps, the success of her fraudulent letter which prompted her to write another. Again, her victim was Isaac Garrett but this time she sought his poison book which contained her historic transactions as Mrs Wood of Hillside. On 14 July, she approached an 11-year-old boy called Adam May who was walking alone along Church Street that afternoon. She asked him to deliver the letter to Garrett's and accompanied him to Queen's Road before continuing to Duke Street, where he was to fetch the book, once he had it in his possession. Back on Queen's Road, Garrett received the following note:

Ship Street, July 1871

Sir, I shall be much obliged if you would allow me the loan of your book wherein you register the poisonous drugs you sell. It is merely in furtherance to an inquiry I am making as to the sale of certain poisons, and bears no reference to anything you have sold or any irregularity in selling, but only to aid me in my investigation. You will tie up your book and send it at once by the bearer: it shall be returned, as you may need it.

Yours truly,
D. Black, Borough Coroner.

Christiana knew that Isaac Garrett was a cautious man and that he would not want to hinder the important work of the borough coroner. Just as she predicted, Garrett immediately tied up his book in paper and handed it to Adam May who then delivered it to Christiana. Curiously, she did not tear out the pages detailing the transactions made by her alter ego, Mrs Wood of Hillside, but instead removed the ones on either side before returning the book to Garrett's shop. The scale and complexity of her poisoning spree tells us that this move was not a mistake on Christiana's behalf. There was method in her madness, even if her motivation is unclear. She perhaps had no desire to cover her tracks at all and tore out the pages simply to amuse herself and puzzle Isaac Garrett. Whatever the truth, her next move is much easier to understand. She decided to stop using strychnine and turned her attentions to arsenic, the nineteenth century poisoner's weapon of choice. Her experiences had taught her that strychnine's bitter taste almost always prevented her victim from ingesting the full dose. In contrast, arsenic is odourless and tasteless, making it impossible for a potential victim to detect in food or drink. On 19 July, she sent a boy to Garrett's with a note purporting to come from Glaisyer and Kemp. But her plan did not work as well as before. This time, Garrett did not provide her with any poison. By now, his suspicions were aroused and he headed directly to the premises of Glaisyer and Kemp to enquire about the note he had received. Worryingly, Thomas Glaisyer had no knowledge of any note requesting two ounces of arsenic and, even worse, he knew nothing about the drachm of strychnine that Garrett had received on 8 June. Panic and concern now set in as Garrett realised that a person had obtained poison from him by deception and he had no idea for what means. He left Glaisyer and Kemp's and headed directly to the police station where he explained to Inspector Gibbs what had happened. Gibbs was confident that Garrett had not committed a crime, having followed the rules of the Pharmacy Act to the letter. But there were pages missing from his poison book, a fact which Garrett could not explain, and no discernible reason why the coroner might need to view his historic transactions. Garrett's narrative left Gibbs feeling baffled but he knew he was on the verge of uncovering his biggest case to date.

While Isaac Garrett had grown wise to Christiana's deception, she didn't have to venture too far to find another chemist who would supply her with arsenic. In 1871 Brighton was home to around fifty-six chemists and druggists[6] and there was one in particular who had become of great interest to Christiana. His name was Samuel Bradbury and she had recently heard that he was due to cease trading and leave Brighton for good. She thus composed a letter to Bradbury, again purporting to come from Glaisyer and Kemp, and requesting three ounces of arsenic. She quickly found a boy to deliver the note to his premises at 21 North Street and he returned within minutes bearing three one-ounce packets of arsenic, enough to kill hundreds of Brighton's unsuspecting public.

A few days later, Christiana received an unexpected letter from Inspector Gibbs. This was her first contact with the inspector since the inquest in June and his letter related to the evidence she had provided, specifically the date she had purchased the creams from John Maynard and had the analysis made by Schweitzer, the chemist. Christiana hoped that this request might be the start of an investigation into John Maynard and she therefore composed a reply straightaway:

> *Miss Edmunds begs to inform Mr Gibbs that she bought the last lot of chocolate creams at Mr Maynard's on the 16th of March and had them analysed the same day at Mr Schweitzer's.*[7]

She decided to deliver the letter to Inspector Gibbs personally and set out for the police station. He was out when she arrived so she left the letter in his office and walked back to Gloucester Place, via the Pavilion grounds, where she met Gibbs unexpectedly. In the conversation that followed, Gibbs informed her that he was investigating a number of new poisoning cases that had come to his attention in the weeks after Sidney Barker's death. There had been no more fatalities, to his knowledge, but each victim had become unwell after eating a chocolate cream from Maynard's. Many of the victims were children, said Gibbs, and he was now in the process of piecing the case together. This was not the information Christiana had hoped for but it still provided an opportunity to slur Maynard's reputation. She reminded Gibbs that she had twice been poisoned by his chocolate creams and that he had barely acknowledged her complaint in March. The inspector thanked Christiana for the information and she departed the Pavilion grounds, none the wiser to the true purpose of his letter or this meeting. Gibbs had an inkling that Christiana was more involved in the poisoning case than first realised. Every victim that he had interviewed in connection with the chocolate creams had mentioned seeing or meeting with a lady and their descriptions matched Christiana perfectly. But he wanted to make certain of her involvement before questioning her further and he headed back to the police station to look over her letter. Once he had studied the handwriting, he took out the forged note given to him by Isaac Garrett and placed it against her letter to make a comparison. He observed some similarities between the two samples but could not be sure if the handwriting belonged to the same person. Fortunately, Gibbs had someone on whom he could call: a handwriting expert who could determine if Christiana was the person at the heart of Brighton's poisoning epidemic.

Chapter Eight

"A Delicate Thing to Allude to"

On the afternoon of Tuesday 8 August, Christiana and her mother left Gloucester Place and travelled to Brighton Rail Station. Christiana was heading to her hometown of Margate and told her mother and friends that she wanted to look over a house and visit Louisa's grave. Ann accompanied her daughter to the rail platform and then returned home, an act which filled her with some trepidation. It was not the journey which worried Ann but her daughter's increasingly fractious and troubled state of mind. She had watched Christiana mentally deteriorate over the last year and knew that her feelings for Dr Beard were the cause of it, though she was powerless to help. For Ann, Christiana's mind was a 'delicate thing to allude to' and she did not discuss it with Dr Beard or any other physician in Brighton. Ann likely feared that Christiana would face a similar fate to her late husband and son and be sent to an asylum, a place synonymous with misery and death in the Edmunds family.

Ann wasn't the only person to be concerned about the ongoing changes to Christiana's state of mind. Alice Over, her former landlady, called at Gloucester Place frequently during this period and, on one occasion, asked Christiana why she seemed so unhappy. She said she felt uncomfortable and as if she were sometimes going mad. There is no evidence to suggest that those closest to Christiana had any knowledge of her poisoning spree but this is hardly surprising; she thrived on the secrets and deception, even though it caused her great anguish. Despite her cunning, one member of her household was starting to become very suspicious. She was the house servant Charlotte, who had observed something strange a few days before the trip to Margate. On the day in question, Christiana had delivered to Charlotte a tray covered in powders, each one in its packet, but partly undone and missing their labels. Christiana instructed her to take the powders away and left without saying anything further. After inspecting the contents of the tray, Charlotte kept one of the packets because she thought it was powdered myrrh, a traditional treatment for skin problems, sore throats and a wide range of other common ailments, but she threw the other powders on the fire. Perhaps after trying the 'myrrh', Charlotte suspected that the powder was not as innocent as first assumed and, sometime later, she handed the packet over to Inspector Gibbs.[1]

In the meantime, Ann was alone at Gloucester Place and hoping that a trip to Margate might bring some much-needed relief to her daughter's mind. If not, she vowed to leave Brighton for good, unless Dr Beard and his wife went first.[2] Had Ann known the real reason for Christiana's visit to Margate, she might have carried out her vow much sooner because it was not about looking at a house or seeing Louisa's grave. It was, in fact, a necessary step in the final phase of her poisoning spree and it began at 19 Albert Terrace, a lodging house owned by a Mrs Bearlings and overlooking the sea only a few minutes away from Christiana's childhood home in Hawley Square. On arrival, Christiana was greeted by Mrs Bearlings' servant, Adelaide, who let her a room for the night at the cost of half a crown and then accompanied her upstairs with her luggage. Christiana said nothing about how long she might stay or why she had travelled to Margate alone and this immediately piqued Adelaide's curiosity. It was unusual to have an unaccompanied lady stay in the house and even her luggage appeared odd to Adelaide: she carried only a small, black, leather bag and a square box wrapped in brown paper and tied up with string. Adelaide did not pry about her stay in Margate but, when she attended Christiana's room the next day, she took her opportunity to learn more about this strange lady visitor. Adelaide knew she shouldn't meddle with her guests' possessions but the large, red box on the table was too intriguing to ignore. When she opened the box, she found two peaches inside and a second box, smaller in size. This box was filled with crystallised sweets and contained a smaller, third box which Adelaide found empty. Seeing nothing else of interest, Adelaide replaced the boxes and left the room before her guest reappeared. Later that evening, Christiana paid for a second night at Mrs Bearlings' and left at 7:30 am on the following morning. She told Adelaide that she would take the 8 am train to Ramsgate but this was a lie: she went first to London before returning to Brighton in the evening. Ann did not collect Christiana from the station but she was met at the gate by the servant Charlotte, who noticed that Christiana had with her the black leather bag, while the box wrapped in brown paper had mysteriously disappeared.

On the afternoon of Friday, 10 August, a railway van delivered a parcel to 64 Grand Parade. It had come from Victoria Station in London with the postage prepaid and was addressed to Mrs Emily Beard. A servant took delivery of the package and took it to her mistress in the sitting room. The package was about a foot in length, neatly wrapped in brown paper and Emily wondered if it might be a gift from Dr Beard who was away in the North. She removed the paper, opened the box and found inside some cakes, preserved fruits and gingerbread nuts. Next to these, Emily saw a plum cake, about the size of a tea cup, with some paper wrapped around it on which the sender had written a message:

'A few home-made cakes for the children; those done up are flavoured on purpose for yourself to enjoy. You will guess who this is from. I can't mystify you, I fear. I hope this will arrive in time for you tonight while the eatables are still fresh.'

Emily did not recognise the handwriting, nor the sender's initials, G.M., but she thought the cakes would make a nice treat for herself and her children on Saturday and she re-wrapped the parcel and left it in the kitchen.

Later that day, the railway van made a second visit to Grand Parade but this time to number 59, the home of Jacob Boys, a retired solicitor, and his family. Emily Helsey, the Boys' parlour maid, took delivery of the parcel that was addressed to her mistress, Elizabeth Boys, and left it on the sideboard in the dining room. When Elizabeth returned home that evening, she opened the parcel and found two pieces of gingerbread, two macaroons, two cheesecakes and two currant cakes. Wrapped separately were two tartlets addressed to her directly, alongside the following handwritten note:

'I send you some cakes for your two little girls. Those directed to yourself are my first efforts. I hope to see you soon. Your old friend – J.N.'

Elizabeth did not recognise the initials nor did she like tartlets but, seeing no harm in the gift, she sent the box and its contents upstairs to her nursemaid with instructions to give them to her daughters, Emily and Gertrude, after lunch the next day

Over the course of Friday, more parcels began to appear across Brighton. On North Street, William Curtis, the editor of the *Brighton Gazette*, received a round box of crystallised sweets. Isaac Garrett, the chemist on Queen's Road, was sent two peaches and a half sovereign with a handwritten note that said: 'The last of my debt and the first of my fruit from my garden.' Across town, George Tatham, a surgeon and borough magistrate, had also received a box of cakes late on Friday evening. Finally, a box was delivered to Christiana at seventeen Gloucester Place, comprising of some strawberries, two peaches and a pair of gloves. None of the recipients could identify the sender nor the reason for the gifts but, by the next day, the case of the mysterious parcels had taken an unexpected turn, beginning first at 59 Grand Parade.

It was 11 pm on Saturday night when a messenger came to the home of Nathaniel Blaker, a surgeon, and informed him of a medical emergency at the home of Elizabeth Boys. Blaker left his house on the Old Steine immediately and made his way to Grand Parade where he found two servants, Amelia Mills and Emily Helsey, suffering from 'considerable collapse, pain and vomiting'.[3] He directed his first attentions to Mill who said to Blaker that she felt 'indescribably ill' after eating a piece of a tartlet earlier that day.[4] It started with a burning in her throat and chest and, by the evening, the nausea, vomiting and trembling had set in. The other servant, Helsey, had experienced similar symptoms but was already beginning to show signs of improvement. Elizabeth Boys confirmed the girls' story and explained to Blaker that the tartlet, and a number of other cakes, had been sent to the house anonymously the day before. Blaker was surprised at the severity of the illness: he thought the fruit inside the tartlet had gone bad and reassured the servants that their symptoms would be short-lived.[5] As there was nothing more he could do, Blaker left the house but promised to return the next day.

Nathaniel Blaker had only taken a few steps along Grand Parade when another servant approached him and asked him to go to Dr Beard's house at number 64. Blaker knew Dr Beard personally, having worked alongside him as a surgeon at the Sussex County Hospital, and headed directly to the house. On arrival, he found two servants, Emily Agate and Margaret Knight, suffering from the exact symptoms he had just observed at the home of Elizabeth Boys. When he spoke with Emily Beard, she related a tale almost identical to Elizabeth Boys: that the servants had become unwell after eating cakes and preserved fruits from an anonymous parcel delivered to the house the day before. Blaker's suspicions now aroused, he examined some of the preserved fruit and found it was coated with a fine layer of white powder. Given the nature of the servants' symptoms, he believed the powder to be a form of irritant poison, perhaps arsenic, but he would need to collect samples and perform an analysis before he could be certain. He gathered as much of the servant's vomit as he could in a clay jar alongside the remaining preserved fruit. He then returned to the Boys' house and collected the same, which he took home and locked in a cupboard for safekeeping.[6]

Blaker barely slept that Saturday night. The more he thought about the events on Grand Parade, the more he considered the possibility of deliberate poisoning. The servants he examined had displayed all of the classic symptoms of arsenic: a burning sensation in the mouth and throat, nausea, intense pain in the gut, followed by a violent purging of the stomach and bowels. It was, of course, possible that the servants had simultaneously experienced a bout of gastroenteritis, dysentery or, perhaps even, cholera, but this explanation did not account for the presence of white powder on the preserved fruit. As soon as the sun rose, Blaker took the samples to the Sussex County Hospital to have them analysed by a colleague called Walter Smith who worked as a chemist in the dispensary and was familiar with poisoning and its detection. He examined first a 1oz piece of cake and quickly discovered that it contained 580mg of arsenic:[7] more than enough to kill two adults.[8] His suspicions now confirmed, Blaker rushed to the police station and informed Inspector Gibbs of what had passed on Grand Parade the previous night and handed over all of the evidence he had collected. From there he returned to the Beard and Boys' household to check on the servants and was relieved to find that all but one had recovered. Amelia Mills, nursemaid to the Boys, remained the worst affected but he felt confident that she would survive this attack and make a full recovery over the next few days.

Back at the police station, Inspector Gibbs had another visitor in reference to the poisoned parcels. His name was Frederick Humphrey and he was a surgeon who had recently attended a lady in Gloucester Place. The address piqued Gibbs' interest because of its association with Christiana Edmunds, the lady whose role in the poisoning investigations he was yet to determine. Humphrey confirmed that Christiana was the patient and he had come to seek assistance from the police because he believed she was the victim of deliberate poisoning. He explained that she had received some fruit on Thursday evening after returning from a visit to Margate. After she ate the fruit, she experienced a burning in her throat, some nausea and vomiting; symptoms which Humphrey attributed to arsenic poisoning. On hearing this news, Gibbs accompanied Humphrey directly Gibbs directly to 17 Gloucester Place. When he entered the house, he found Christiana lying on a couch, looking tired and very pale. She greeted him by saying 'here I am again, Mr Gibbs, nearly poisoned!' As Christiana described the arrival of the mysterious parcel, her mother handed a green box to the inspector that was addressed to Miss Christina [sic] Edmunds. As he examined the box, Christiana continued: 'It came on Thursday evening, about 7.30 by post. It is evidently from someone in the town, for it bears the Brighton post-mark and it is evident that it is no one acquainted with me or they would have known my address or how to spell my name properly.' The box was now empty but Christiana informed him that it had contained some strawberries, two apricots and a new pair of gloves.

'And what became of the contents?' asked Inspector Gibbs.

'Mrs Edmunds ate the strawberries. I ate one apricot, and that was all right but the next was very bitter and I spat it all out, and have been ill ever since.'

Here, Ann spoke to confirm her daughter's story. She told Gibbs that after spitting out the piece of apricot, Christiana went to take another bite but Ann compelled her to stop and reminded her of the 'little boy Barker' who had so tragically lost his life a few months earlier.[9] Not long after, Christiana became unwell and Ann had called on Mr Humphrey to attend to her daughter. She had called on Dr Beard first but he refused to come, a fact Ann kept to herself. When Christiana casually asked about Emily Beard, Gibbs revealed no details but only mentioned that she, Elizabeth Boys and William Curtis had received boxes. Christiana's parting words taunted Inspector Gibbs: 'How very strange! I feel certain you'll never find it out.'[10]

The inspector's suspicions towards Christiana had grown considerably over the last few weeks and her last words only made him more determined to prove her involvement, whatever it may be. He removed from the parcels the address labels and the notes inside and sent them to Frederick Netherclift, the handwriting expert. Gibbs had no other leads and the police came under intense scrutiny as the public panicked amid talk of widespread poisoning. The summer season was Brighton's busiest time of year and the authorities were keen to solve the case before it impacted on the town's tourist trade. The Chief Inspector of the Brighton Police, George White, took personal control of the case and launched a public appeal for information, beginning with this notice that he placed in the *Brighton Gazette* on 12 August:

Borough of Brighton – Twenty Pounds Reward.
Whereas some evil predisposed person has lately sent to different families in Brighton parcels of fruit, cakes and sweets, which have been found to contain poison. Notice is hereby given, that whoever will give such INFORMATION to the undersigned as shall lead to apprehension and conviction of the offender will be paid a reward of £20.
By order of the Watch Committee,
George White – Chief Constable.[11]

The notice makes clear popular feeling to the perpetrator, an 'evil predisposed person', who continued to evade detection. That the Watch Committee were willing to pay such a high reward, the equivalent of £1,000 today, demonstrates the severity and urgency of the situation.

The sensational nature of the crime enabled White's words to spread quickly around the country and it was picked up first by *The Times* who printed the notice alongside details of the parcels and their contents. Within days of issuing the notice, Dr Beard came forward as a witness. He had been away in the North when the anonymous parcel was delivered to his home on 10 August but returned to Brighton as soon as Emily wrote to inform him of the events that weekend. This second attempt on Emily's life convinced Dr Beard that Christiana was the perpetrator and he felt compelled to share this information with the police, for fear that she might strike a third time. At the police station, he had a private interview with Inspector Gibbs, in which he related the complete history of his relationship with Christiana Edmunds. It was not easy for Dr Beard to relate such personal details. While he stressed that his feelings for Christiana were purely platonic, he knew that any hint of extra-marital romance risked subjecting his entire family to scandal, especially if these details were ever made public. This fear, he explained to Inspector Gibbs, also accounted for his reason to not report to the police Christiana's first attempt on Emily's life back in September 1870. In addition, he had no evidence to support his claim, there were no credible witnesses to the event and Ann Edmunds had hinted at the possibility of legal action, should he take the matter any further. Believing there was little more he could do, Dr Beard put his wife on her guard and ceased all contact with the Edmunds family.

For Inspector Gibbs, this fascinating narrative confirmed every one of his suspicions about Christiana and convinced him that she was the perpetrator of the poisoned parcel that was delivered to Emily Beard. Dr Beard's testimony also provided a plausible motive: Christiana had attempted to murder Emily so she could see have Dr Beard for herself. But what of the other victims? To Gibbs' knowledge, Christiana and Elizabeth Boys were not acquainted nor was she a friend to William Curtis, the editor of the *Brighton Gazette*. It made little sense that she would target strangers in such a personal manner but then again, this may have been a deliberate move to misdirect the police's attention and ensure that the finger of suspicion did not point in her direction. This would also explain why she sent a parcel to herself and allegedly ate its contents. That she targeted high-profile families also suggests that Christiana wanted to finally bring her crimes to public notice and ensure that she received the attention she so desired. Gibbs did not yet know about the parcels received by the magistrate, George Tatham, and the chemist, Isaac Garrett, but interest in the case only heightened as these additional victims became known.

Gibbs took Dr Beard's information directly to Chief Inspector White who immediately issued a warrant for Christiana's arrest. She was to be charged with the attempted murder of Emily Beard but the police needed more evidence from the other victims before they could bring additional charges against her. White accompanied Gibbs to Gloucester Place on 17 August to take Christiana into custody and she neither admitted nor denied her role in the crime: 'Me poison Mrs Beard? Who can say that? I have been nearly poisoned myself!'[12] From Gloucester Place, Christiana was taken to Lewes Prison where she spent the night in custody, ready to face the borough magistrates in the morning. Her arrest had brought the poisoning spree to an end but the police now faced the enormous task of gathering the necessary evidence to secure her committal to trial and, later, her conviction. Some witnesses had already come forward but Gibbs and his colleagues did not yet appreciate the complexity and extent of her crimes. The truth about Christiana Edmunds would dramatically reveal itself in the coming weeks and secure her reputation as Brighton's infamous Chocolate Cream Killer.

Chapter Nine

"Most Extraordinary and Most Serious Charges"

At 11 am on Friday, 18 August, Christiana Edmunds was taken from prison to the Brighton Police Court, a large room in the basement of the Town Hall. This was the first step in the Victorian judicial process: a hearing before the magistrates to determine if Christiana would stand trial for the crime of poisoning Emily Beard. Though she had spent less than twenty-four hours in custody, the news of her arrest had already spread across Brighton and the courtroom was crowded with journalists and members of the public who had arrived long before the proceedings began, eager to hear every detail of the case. As Christiana entered the court and took her seat in the dock, much was made of her personal appearance and social background. The *Daily News* noted that she wore a black silk dress, black lace shawl and black veiled bonnet[1] and *The Manchester Times* found her very ladylike in her demeanour, though not of a 'very prepossessing appearance'.[2] In contrast, the *Evening Gazette* highlighted her 'fair complexion' and found her 'good looking'.[3] Despite being described as 35-years-old in newspaper reports, Christiana was, in fact, 43 at the time of her hearing and keen to conceal her true age to the hordes of male journalists.

In the dock, Christiana 'bowed and smiled at her friends' who sat beneath her[4] and was especially pleased to see her sister, Mary, who had travelled from Lancing in West Sussex to be in court. Christiana's behaviour suggests that she was completely unaware of her the gravity of her situation. The press called the hearing one of the 'most extraordinary and most serious charges ever brought before a court of justice'[5] and for good reason. Of all the weapons available to the budding murderess, poison was, by far, the most feared and abhorred in Victorian England. Though the majority of poisonings in this period were accidental or suicidal, vivid and dramatic tales of deliberate poisoning, especially by arsenic, had come to dominate the newspapers and capture the public's imagination, creating a moral panic that endured throughout the century. While the introduction of legislation to control the sale of poison had allayed some of these fears, the Victorians remained unable to eradicate cases of deliberate poisoning and to destroy poison's cultural reputation as an instrument of 'death and agony'.[6]

That poisoning came to be associated with women was another reason for the fear which accompanied this crime. The Victorians idealised women as 'angels of the hearth': nurturing and caring beings who devoted themselves to child-rearing and matters of the home. When a woman committed poisoning, it contravened these well-defined, though restrictive, notions of femininity, making the crime unexpected and therefore all the more shocking. Cases of female-perpetrated poisoning made for exciting reading but raised questions about women's domestic role, as one journalist from *The Times* lamented in 1849: 'It seems almost clear that a woman who would not lift her hand against a man or child will unhesitatingly drop arsenic into their food'. Of course, the reality of poisoning was far different: only 254 women stood accused of murder and attempted murder by poison for the entire period of 1750–1914[7], a relatively small figure, but these cultural anxieties set the scene for Christiana's hearing and her treatment by the press.

The proceedings opened with the testimony of Emily Beard who related a full account of her friendship with Christiana Edmunds, including the poisoning attempt in September 1870 and the poisoned parcel which was delivered to her home on 10 August. In discussing these events, Emily was forced to reveal the extent of Christiana's feelings towards her husband; a difficult task in such a public forum. Even more humiliating, the letter which Christiana had written to Dr Beard after Sidney Barker's inquest was read aloud by the prosecutor, William Stuckey. This evidence scandalised the Beards but it was necessary, said Stuckey, in establishing a motive: that Christiana had poisoned Emily in order to have Dr Beard for herself. This was convincing evidence and Charles Lamb, the man tasked with defending Christiana, had only one question to ask Emily Beard in his cross-examination: was she certain that the poisoned chocolate cream of September 1870 had come from Christiana's pocket? Emily could not state definitively if Christiana had taken it from her pocket or had not;[8] but her uncertainty was not enough to concern the prosecution.

Over the next few hours, the court heard from two of Emily Beard's servants, Emily Agate and Margaret Knight, and the surgeon, Nathaniel Paine Blaker, who all testified to the ill-effects of the cakes sent to Grand Parade. Next, Isaac Garrett produced the forged notes he had received purporting to come from the coroner, David Black, and the chemists, Glaisyer and Kemp. As the police investigation into Christiana was still ongoing, William Stuckey asked the court to adjourn the proceedings for one week. His request was granted but Christiana was denied bail and instead returned to the prison at nearby Lewes, though the magistrate granted her a visit with her mother and sister.

Back in Brighton, the adjournment gave the police the opportunity to continue with their enquiries. Chief Inspector White focused on finding the boys who had delivered the forged notes on Christiana's behalf. He issued notices around the town urging anybody with information to come forward, in the hope that someone might be able to positively identify her in court. Inspector Gibbs was busy too, with preparations for the chemical analysis which, the police hoped, would provide conclusive proof of the presence of arsenic in the victims' fruits and cakes. On 23 August, he travelled to London to deliver four jars of evidence to Julian Rodgers, a surgeon and professor of toxicology at the London Hospital. The first jar contained some cake and fruit from the poisoned parcels, the second and third had inside the vomit of two of the servants and a handkerchief collected from Nathaniel Blaker was placed in the fourth. As soon as the delivery was made, Gibbs returned directly to Brighton, ready for the proceedings to resume the next day.

Once again, the court was filled with press and spectators long before the hearing commenced at 11 am on Thursday 24 August. Christiana was again occupied in passing notes to her sister as the prosecutor rose and stated that he had new evidence to present against her. It was his belief that Christiana had procured a large quantity of poison under a false name and was responsible for a number of poisoning attacks that had occurred in Brighton over recent months. This immediately prompted an objection from Charles Lamb who complained of the 'general evidence' presented by the prosecution in relation to Christiana's 'dealings with poison'. He believed that the court should only hear evidence in support of the charge of poisoning Emily Beard with arsenic and anything else should be ruled inadmissible. In other words, Lamb feared that additional charges would be levelled against Christiana and that he would be unable to provide an adequate defence. Lamb was immediately overruled by John Merrifield, the stipendiary magistrate, and the prosecution called its first witness.

When Adam May stepped into the witness box, Christiana realised that the police had uncovered the full extent of her poisoning spree. Adam May was the boy who took the forged notes to Isaac Garett's in July to obtain the poison book and he revealed every detail of his meeting with Christiana in court. But when William Stuckey asked Adam if the lady he met was today present in court, he said he could not be sure. This was a small victory for the defence but the prosecution's next witness, Harriett Cole, knew Christiana personally and swore to seeing her and Adam May walking together along Queen's Road. Harriett

Cole was an unexpected addition to the proceedings. When Christiana had visited her shop at the beginning of June and left a bag of poisoned chocolate creams in a zinc pail by the door, she thought that nobody had seen her. But Harriett Cole had observed the drop and became suspicious of Christiana after her daughter became unwell later that day. She explained to the court that she next saw Christiana at Sidney Barker's inquest where she asked her about the chocolate creams. Christiana denied all knowledge and Harriett remained suspicious but did not take the matter any further. Her testimony was corroborated by Caroline Walker, another victim of the chocolate creams left at the grocer's shop, and William Moon, a boy who delivered a forged note to Isaac Garrett's for the purpose of procuring poison. Unlike Adam May, William identified Christiana as the lady who had given him the note and pointed directly to her in the court room.[9]

The prosecution's case against Christiana now overwhelmed the defence. Once again, Lamb objected to the 'general evidence' presented by William Stuckey but his objections were overruled by the magistrate. Over the course of the day, the court heard damning testimony from Isaac Garrett and Caroline Stone about Christiana's purchases of strychnine, under the false name of Mrs Wood, and from Charlotte Pettit and Adelaide Friend, who described Christiana's trip to Margate and the mysterious box that had accompanied her. Lamb's fears were realised when the prosecution warned Christiana of the possibility of additional charges as the evidence-gathering continued. Unsurprisingly, she was refused bail when the proceedings were adjourned at 5:10 pm and spent another week in Lewes Prison.[10]

Despite the increasing severity of her situation, Christiana appeared 'cheerful' at the next court session on Thursday, 31 August. She wore a bonnet of bright blue, decorated with a white rose and bowed at her friends and family as she took her seat in the dock. She surveyed the court with 'apparent unconcern' and was again supplied with a pencil and paper to pass notes to her friends and to her solicitor. After some hushed discussion with the bench, William Stuckey declared that Christiana would be additionally charged with the attempted murder by poison of Elizabeth Boys and Isaac Garrett, charges which prompted shock among the spectators. Lamb immediately protested but, as the prosecution explained, new evidence had come to light that would demonstrate Christiana's guilt and he called the handwriting expert, Frederick Netherclift, to the witness box

By 1871, graphology, or the study of handwriting, had become a common feature in English criminal proceedings and Frederick Netherclift was one of the finest in his field. He had been trained in handwriting analysis by his father, the late Joseph Netherclift, who was widely regarded as the country's first expert and had begun testifying in criminal trials in the 1830s. Like his father, Netherclift was a lithographer by trade: a printer who made copies of documents and images by tracing the original onto a prepared surface and using an ink roller to take an impression. It was through the tracing process that Netherclift, and his father before him, had become intimately acquainted with the 'peculiarities of handwriting',[11] and had learned how to distinguish one person's hand from another. By the time of Christiana's hearing, Netherclift had thirty years of experience in handwriting analysis and claimed to have given evidence 'to almost every court in England'.[12] Because of the nature of his profession, Netherclift often appeared in cases of suspected forgeries and inheritance disputes. His most famous case to-date was that of William Roupell, the former Member of Parliament for Lambeth who faced trial in 1862. Roupell was the illegitimate son of Richard Palmer Roupell, a wealthy merchant, who had invested heavily in property and land. Roupell had squandered a fortune and amassed a great debt as he sought to establish himself in society. To solve his financial problems, he set about forging documents in order to obtain by deception the lion's share of his father's property. He even destroyed his father's will and composed a new one in which he disinherited his brother, Richard, and made himself the executor.

His father died in 1856 and, by 1862, Roupell could no longer pay the mortgages on his numerous properties and fled to Spain. He was prosecuted for fraud on his return to England and sentenced to penal servitude for fourteen years. But the case went to court on a further two occasions as Roupell's brother, Richard, sought to reclaim what he believed was his rightful inheritance. The prosecution called Netherclift to examine the deeds to the properties in question and he confirmed that they were all forged by Roupell. In light of his evidence, the jury could not agree on what constituted Richard's inheritance and he spent the rest of his life trying to recover his father's fortune.[13]

Netherclift's involvement in the Roupell case brought him to national attention and his remit of cases began to widen. Whether the charge was fraud or attempted murder, he prepared for each case in the same way, with a careful analysis of the samples forwarded to him by the authorities. For Christiana's hearing, he had analysed the address labels on the poisoned parcels and the forged letters sent to Isaac Garrett. For the purposes of comparison, the prosecution had sent to him a letter written by Christiana, likely the one she wrote to Dr Beard after the inquest. In court, the prosecution asked Netherclift about the process of examination:

William Stuckey: Is it the general characteristics in the handwriting you go upon?

Frederick Netherclift: Certainly; style is a different thing altogether. Handwriting may be written either upright or sloping; we therefore look for characteristics.

Stuckey: How do you generally proceed?

Netherclift: I first of all examine the admitted handwriting and pick out some 12 or 14 of its peculiarities. I then compare that handwriting with the disguised, and if I find it to contain the same characteristics I consider I have good ground for believing them to be the same handwriting.[14]

Netherclift stated that after a 'careful and minute examination' on these points, he became 'firmly convinced' that the same person had composed each of the samples and that a deliberate attempt had been made to disguise the handwriting of the address labels and the forged letters. But, in an attempt to discredit Netherclift, Lamb showed him the poison book from Isaac Garrett's shop and asked him to comment on two signatures made by Caroline Stone, the milliner. Netherclift noted that the two signatures were different and Lamb asked if they were at all alike. He replied 'I should not like to say they were written by the same person unless I had half an hour's examination and compared them with other specimens of her handwriting. I would not undertake to give an off-hand opinion upon them'. But Lamb persisted in this subject:

Charles Lamb: Would you pledge your reputation that they are written by the same person?

Frederick Netherclift: – I refuse to give an opinion without comparing them with other signatures. If you want an opinion with reference to them you can have it by giving me time and furnishing me with other signatures but I shall expect my fees!

Netherclift's remarks caused laughter in the courtroom. In his thirty years of giving evidence, he had faced many attempts to discredit his analysis but he knew too well how to handle the likes of Charles Lamb. He had faced a similar situation eight years earlier, during his cross-examination in the Roupell Forgery case, prompting him to make the most famous assertion of his career: that he could copy a signature so perfectly that his own father, the great expert, would be 'bothered' by it. The prosecutor tried then to mock him: 'And between you, I suppose, you could have bothered a good many people?' Netherclift's reply was short but enough to silence the prosecutor: 'No doubt'.[15]

Back in the Brighton courtroom, one of the magistrates rose to remind the court that the Lord Chief Justice, Sir Alexander Cockburn, had recently paid 'one of the highest compliments he possibly could' to Netherclift, in remarking that 'he had never yet found him wrong in his life'.[16] Such high praise immediately silenced Charles Lamb and the proceedings turned next to the much-anticipated results of the chemical analysis.

After receiving the jars of evidence from Inspector Gibbs, Professor Julian Rodgers carried out a careful analysis of their contents. With over thirty years' experience in toxicology, Rodgers was well-experienced in the detection of poison and had appeared as an expert witness in a number of criminal proceedings. In his most recent case, Rodgers exonerated the wife of Thomas Pownall, a retired colonel in the army, from the charge of murdering her husband by poison.[17] One year earlier, in November 1869, Rodgers' solved the mysterious deaths of two young children, Emily and Charles Baronius. A post-mortem had failed to ascertain the cause of death and the coroner called on Rodgers to investigate. He found that a batch of contaminated mussels, still present in the stomach, had caused the untimely death of the two children.[18] In contrast, the case of Christiana Edmunds was considerably more straightforward because very little effort, he said, had been made to disguise the poison. In the first jar, for example, Rodgers found cakes sprinkled with a 'most dangerous quantity' of arsenic and one piece of the preserved fruit had been 'literally stuffed' with it. Of the fresh fruit, the peaches had begun to decompose but this only highlighted the appearance of white powder on the surface which Rodgers identified as strychnine. Although he had not yet calculated exact quantities, he was confident that each item contained enough poison to kill its intended victim. The vomit collected from the servants and placed into the second and third jars also revealed dangerous levels of arsenic and he even found trace amounts on the handkerchief. The evidence against Christiana was now so overwhelming that Charles

Lamb did not even attempt a cross-examination of Professor Rodgers.[19] Only Christiana appeared unmoved by his evidence: 'she made no sign of fear and was ... the least excited person in the court', wrote one reporter from the *Morning Post*.[20]

As the day in court drew to a close, the prosecution made its first mention of the case of Sidney Barker, specifically the exoneration of George Ware, the man who supplied the chocolate creams to Maynard's shop. While the coroner had declared Sidney's death to be accidental, the investigation into Christiana and her criminal activities had prompted the authorities to open a fresh inquiry into the events of 12 June. Behind the scenes, the police had re-interviewed the witnesses and successfully tracked down two more of Christiana's errand boys, who had purchased chocolate creams on her behalf around the time of Sidney's death. The police had also submitted the anonymous letters sent to Sidney's father to Frederick Netherclift for handwriting analysis. Over the course of Thursday 7 and Friday 8 September, the court heard how Christiana had sent Adam May, William Guy, and George Brooks to Maynard's shop to purchase chocolate creams. Two of Maynard's assistants, Kate Page and Annie Meadows, recalled that the creams had been returned to the shop and later sold to Charles Miller, Sidney's uncle. The court also listened to the testimony of Christiana's early victims, Benjamin Coultrop and Emily Baker, who had been poisoned with strychnine and positively identified Christiana as the lady responsible. Finally, Frederick Netherclift confirmed that Christiana was the author of the anonymous letters sent to Sidney's father, Albert.[21]

Only one piece of the puzzle remained: what had inspired Christiana to commit such a crime? William Stuckey believed he had the answer and reminded the court of the evidence provided by Emily Beard in which she stated that Christiana had developed an unhealthy obsession with her husband and had tried to poison her back in September 1870. Now, Stuckey called on Dr Beard to confirm his wife's story and provide further proof of a motive. In his examination, Beard testified that he had received many intimate letters from Christiana but had ceased all contact after the attempt on his wife's life. This, Stuckey argued, inspired Christiana to commit mass poisoning in order to 'show the possibility of the sweets being poisoned not by her but by someone else'. During cross-examination, Charles Lamb attempted to show that Christiana's affections for Dr Beard were not wholly unrequited:

Charles Lamb: Did you take any means to prevent letters being sent to you?

Dr Beard: I took no action in the matter to prevent letters being sent.

Lamb: Can you give any reasons why you did not take those means?

Beard: No.

Lamb: Did the prisoner ever give you letters when you were on terms of intimacy with her for you to read when you got home? Did she give you these letters when you were leaving her house?

Beard: She has done so, but I cannot say how often.[22]

Whatever the truth of their relationship, Lamb's examination of Dr Beard did not detract from the overwhelming evidence against Christiana. With the evidence brought to a close, the magistrates had no doubt that she should face trial for the murder of Sidney Barker and the attempted murder of Emily Beard, Elizabeth Boys and Isaac Garrett. Her friends and family wept at the verdict while Christiana remained 'perfectly calm and self-possessed'.[23]

Outside the court, hundreds of members of the public had assembled, anxious to catch a glimpse of the lady poisoner. The hearing had transformed Christiana into the most infamous person in Brighton, if not in the country. In court, William Stuckey had been asked by Dr James Edmunds, a surgeon from London, to publicly announce that he was not a relation of Christiana's,[24] for fear of a taint by association. All over England, caricatures circulated of her image while stories of her criminal deeds filled the newspapers. Behind the headlines, however, some of her victims struggled under the intense media spotlight. The Beards fled Brighton for a new life in Scotland and Isaac Garrett battled to save his reputation. Julius Schweitzer, the chemist who analysed the chocolate creams on Christiana's behalf, accused Garrett of being negligent in his sale of poisons and published his criticisms in the *Pharmaceutical Journal*. The following week Garrett responded with indignation:

It is a golden rule that a man should not be condemned without evidence, and a fair opportunity of explanation or justification. As regards my shop, its situation, extent, position and arrangement, I cannot believe Mr Schweitzer ignorant and I freely offer to him and my fellow tradesmen, the whole for their inspection, and am content to abide their decision. I really cannot at present see why I am to be made a scapegoat; but if my fellow chemists think me worthy of my townsmen's contempt, I must bear the infliction with what grace I may. A little poisoned fruit sent to me another time may prove more effectual.[25]

As her victims began to put their lives back together, Christiana returned to Lewes Prison and began the two-month wait to face trial at the winter session of the Sussex assizes. In the meantime, she was one of 106 men and women incarcerated at Lewes[26] and her charges were among the most serious of any prisoner, past and present. From the time of her arrival, Christiana had received treatment from the prison surgeon for an ailment of a 'peculiar mental character,'[27] possibly resulting from hysteria but certainly not arising from an admission of guilt. During her time at Lewes, Christiana did not confess to the crimes she had committed nor demonstrate any remorse for the hurt she had caused. Whatever the cause of her mental distress, her anxieties centred on physical appearance and the governor granted her some 'trifling exceptions' on the recommendation of the prison surgeon. She was allowed to wear her own dresses, instead of the prison-issued uniform, and to wear a bonnet to services in the chapel. In every other respect, however, Christiana did not receive any special treatment and was expected to conform to the prison's rules and regulations.[28]

Like other female prisoners, Christiana occupied a single cell in the women's section of the prison. The cell contained a hammock, mattress, pillow and blanket for sleeping and some items to keep it clean, including some rags and a dustpan and brush. She was also issued with some personal items, including a soap-tin and a comb, alongside utensils for eating, as all meals were taken inside the cell.[29] Under the orders of the governor, Christiana was not allowed to use cutlery unless supervised by a prison officer, as a 'precaution against any mischief'.[30]

Life at Lewes was strictly regulated with the day beginning at 5.30 am. Inside the cell, prisoners received a pail of water for washing and a breakfast of bread and gruel before starting the day's activities. There was some opportunity for exercise outside in the yard and morning prayers held in the chapel. Prisoners were expected to work during the day and the men, at least, were involved in the laborious task of untwisting lengths of old rope, known as picking oakum.[31] There are no records relating to Christiana's stay in Lewes but it is unlikely that her mental illness precluded her from some type of work. She may have worked in the prison laundry, a common place of employment for female prisoners. Either way, this was the first time that Christiana had ever occupied her day with any form of manual labour; a shock for a lady of independent means. Once the day's work was complete, prisoners returned to their cell for a final meal of bread and water before the bell rang at 8 pm to signal the time for bed.[32]

Outside of the prison, popular feeling against Christiana intensified as her trial date neared. On 5 November, the Lewes Bonfire Society, an organisation with over 1,000 members, burned an effigy of Christiana in the public square. This protest had the support of 'many gentlemen' in the district and it was now feared that an unbiased jury could not be found for Christiana's trial. As a result, an application was made to the Brighton Police Court to have the trial removed to the Central Criminal Court, or Old Bailey, in London.[33] This was not the first time that such an application had been made: in fact, Parliament had passed the Central Criminal Court Act in 1856 for this specific purpose. It was inspired by the trial of William Palmer, a surgeon and notorious gambler who stood accused of poisoning his friend, John Parsons Cook, at the Shrewsbury Races in November 1855. Thanks to the Act, Palmer's trial was removed from his home county of Staffordshire to the Old Bailey where he was found guilty of murder and sentenced to death on 27 May 1856. Palmer was returned to Staffordshire for his execution by hanging on 14 June.

When the Sussex assizes met on 22 December 1871, Christiana's case was the fourth to be heard and four true bills were presented against her: one for murder and three for attempted murder. The Judge, Baron Martin, agreed to remove the trial from Lewes to the Old Bailey and set the date for 8 January 1872. Back at Lewes, the arrangements for Christiana's departure were made and she travelled by train to London on 28 December 1871. She was incarcerated at the infamous Newgate Prison, adjacent to the Old Bailey, and prepared for the trial which would determine the rest of her life.

Chapter Ten

"The Border Land Between Crime and Insanity"

Newgate Prison was London's most notorious house of correction, famously described in *Moll Flanders* as a place of 'hellish noise' and 'nastiness' that made it feel like an entrance into hell. [1] Opened in the twelfth century, Newgate had housed some of history's most famous criminals, including the great adventurer and bigamist, Casanova, and the highwayman, Dick Turpin. By the time of Christiana's arrival, the prison had been destroyed and rebuilt four times over and was in a considerably better state than in previous centuries, having undergone major reforms as well as significant remodelling between 1858 and 1861. These renovations included a complete overhaul of the women's section of the prison; a separate and self-contained wing to the right of the main entrance and comprising fifty-eight cells over three rows marked B, C, and D; an outside yard, a visiting area and the chapel. There were also two private rooms for prisoners on remand to converse with their solicitor, as they awaited trial at the Old Bailey.

Untouched by these renovations, Newgate's main entrance remained a daunting sight, described here by two visitors to the prison in 1862:

We enter the lodge of Newgate jail by a door, elevated a few steps above the level of the street ... flanked by dark huge masses of stone, forming part of the wall, which is about four feet thick. This outer door is only about four feet and a half high, and is covered on top with formidable iron spikes, the open space above being farther fenced with two strong

iron bars with transverse iron rods. There is another massive oaken inner
door alongside, faced with iron, of enormous strength ... This door has a
very strong Bramah lock with a big brazen bolt, which gives a peculiarly
loud rumbling sound when the key is turned; and at night is secured with
strong iron bolts and padlocks, and by an iron chain.[2]

Christiana had scarcely passed through this formidable entrance when
she demanded an interview with the prison's authorities to protest
her 'improper treatment' at Newgate. She claimed that her furs and
velvet dresses, brought with her from Lewes, had been confiscated
and she was no longer allowed to wear her bonnet to services in the
chapel. At the interview, Edmund Jonas, the governor of Newgate,
pointed out to Christiana that he could not change prison regulations
to 'suit the conveniences of any person' and he advised her to conform
to the rules. He did, however, assure Christiana that he would do
'everything consistent with his duty' to secure her comfort. Christiana
also requested that she be attended by the chaplain of Lewes Prison, a
man who had shown her 'great kindness' during her incarceration in
Sussex. This request raised no objections from Newgate's chaplain,
the Reverend Lloyd Jones, but he asked Christiana to consider that it
might not be easy for him to leave behind his many responsibilities at
Lewes to visit her frequently in London. She, however, could not be
appeased: as a lady, she said, it would be impossible for her to submit to
these rules and she continued to complain to anyone who would listen,
including the Alderman and the Sheriffs of London.[3]

After her interview with the governor and the chaplain, Christiana
was escorted to her cell where her complaints continued. It was not
the cell nor its condition which bothered her but rather the prison's
choice of cellmate: a woman called Eva Pierlo who was on remand
pending trial for bigamy. Perhaps if Christiana had listened to Eva's
tale, she might have had more sympathy for the woman who shared
her cell. Eva was a native of Hamburg who had moved to London and

married Albert Pierlo in December 1870. Albert was a drunk and a gambler who mistreated and physically abused his new wife. He also extorted money from her; taking first a personal allowance of up to 17 shillings per weeks before squandering £80 of her savings on a failed business venture in Hamburg. When the couple returned to London, Albert pawned her best clothing and then disappeared, leaving Eva in a state of personal and financial ruin. Within a few months of Albert's departure, a man called William White heard Eva's tale of woe and offered his hand in marriage. Eva accepted his offer and the pair were married in London on 30 August 1871, but, when Albert heard the news, he contacted the police and Eva was arrested and charged with bigamy and taken to Newgate pending trial.[4]

That a woman accused of murder would complain about sharing a cell with a bigamist seems hardly believable, but Christiana genuinely felt that Eva Pierlo was a person of low moral character whose company and influence should be avoided at all cost. This irony was not lost on the national press who published every detail of Christiana's complaints and treatment in Newgate. Journalists universally pitied its governor, Edmund Jonas, and his unenviable task of managing such a high-profile and high-needs prisoner while under the intense glare of the media.[5] But Jonas was unfazed by Christiana and her endless demands; he ignored her request for a new cellmate and she was left in her cell, measuring seven feet wide and thirteen feet long,[6] to welcome in the New Year of 1872.

In between the visits to chapel, free time in the yard and general life inside the cell, Christiana prepared for her trial, arguably the most important event of her life. She met with John Humffreys Parry, a barrister specially retained by her mother, who worked on building her defence. Parry was a well-respected and highly-experienced barrister whose career in the civil courts had begun in 1843. After his appointment as serjeant-at-law in 1856, Parry became famed for his 'admirable appearance, great clearness and simplicity of statement'[7] and featured in some of the era's most sensational cases. In 1849, for example, he defended Marie Manning, a domestic servant who, alongside her husband, was accused of the murder of her lover, Patrick O'Connor. Parry claimed that Manning was not subject to the jurisdiction of the English court because she was a native of Switzerland. The evidence against her, however, was so overwhelming that the judge found her guilty and sentenced the Mannings to death in October 1849. Parry fared better six years later, in 1855, when he defended William Pierce, one of the three men implicated in the Great Bullion Robbery, a crime in which £12,000 of gold bars and coins were stolen during transportation from London to Paris via train. Pierce was a former railway employee who had played a major role in the planning and execution of the robbery but served only two years in prison. His two accomplices were not so fortunate; they were transported to Australia for fourteen years. But the most sensational case of Parry's career was yet to come. In May 1871, just months before he met Christiana, Parry was involved in the case of Thomas Ernest Boulton and William Park, a transvestite duo known as Fanny and Stella. Parry was retained to defend Park, who alongside Boulton, was accused of conspiring to commit homosexuality. The prosecution collapsed when doctors failed to provide medical evidence of sodomy and the pair were instead charged with indecency, though later found not guilty.

For Parry, the case of Christiana Edmunds was every bit as serious as the Manning murder and equally as shocking as Fanny and Stella. But the more Parry reviewed the evidence, the more baffled he became by Christiana's motive. After much deliberation, he concluded that Christiana was insane at the time she committed the poisonings and he used this belief as the basis of her defence. In order to prove insanity, however, Parry had to satisfy the McNaughtan Rules, the most influential and widely-quoted test for criminal insanity. These rules were based on the case of Daniel McNaughtan, a wood turner from Glasgow, who shot and fatally wounded Edward Drummond, the prime minister's secretary, in 1843. McNaughtan had, in fact, intended to the kill the prime minister because he believed himself to be a victim of persecution by the Tory government. He was acquitted on the grounds of insanity and his case established the tests by which a defendant could be properly judged criminally insane. In essence, the rule states that the 'jurors ought to be told in all cases that every man is to be presumed sane, and to possess a sufficient degree of reason to be responsible for his crimes, until the contrary be proved to their satisfaction'.[8] In other words, if Parry was to convince the jury of Christiana's insanity, he would need to present to the court irrefutable proof of mental illness. If he could not, she would be tried as a sane woman and risked facing the death sentence for her crimes.

Parry's next move, then, was to arrange a meeting between Christiana and some of the country's leading authorities on insanity. In attendance at the meeting were Edmund Jonas, the governor of Newgate and the prison's surgeon, John Rowland Gibson, alongside William Wood, a physician at St Luke's Hospital in London; Henry Maudsley, psychiatrist and professor of medical jurisprudence at University College in London, and Charles Lockhart Robertson, the former superintendent of the Sussex County Asylum and the Court of Chancery's appointed visitor to lunatics. Maudsley and Robertson were also the joint editors of the Journal of Mental Science, known today as the British Journal of Psychiatry, and were well-known and highly-respected figures in the study of madness.

When the experts sat down with Christiana, on 7 January 1872, they were immediately struck by her 'absolute indifference' to her position. William Wood could not 'impress upon her' the severity of the charges and quickly came to the conclusion that Christiana could not distinguish between right and wrong. This view was shared by Henry Maudsley, who found Christiana to be lacking in any moral feeling, and by Charles Lockhart Robertson, who regarded her as 'one of those persons ... on the border land between crime and insanity'.[9] This was

Robertson's second interview with Christiana and it convinced him completely of her insanity. Later that day, he compiled a short memo in which he summarised his thoughts on Christiana. It was later printed in *The Times* and offers a rare glimpse into her state of mind:

> *The most marked symptom is the utter insensibility shown by the prisoner* [Christiana] *to the position she is placed in and the danger she runs. Her whole mind is centred on her letters to Dr Beard, on his conduct in allowing his wife to read them after all that had passed between them, and on the horror she would feel, not at being tried for murder, but at these letters being read in her hearing in court. She further dwelt on her certain belief that Dr Beard desired the death of his wife even by poison; that, though too cautious to speak of it directly, he had hinted at it; and that if so she knew he would marry her. There was no emotion or anguish shown during my two searching examinations.*
>
> *From these facts I conclude that, while the prisoner has in the abstract without question the knowledge of right and wrong, and knows that to poison is to commit murder, she is so devoid of all sense of moral responsibility that she cannot be regarded as conscious of right or wrong, or morally responsible, in the sense which other men are so. Her family history of insanity, epilepsy and idiocy points to the insane temperament and is consistent with the deduction that the prisoner is morally insane.*[10]

The term 'moral insanity' was a familiar one in the later nineteenth century. It was defined as a 'morbid perversion of the natural feelings' and caused a person to behave irrationally and antisocially, often with a strong propensity to violence or mischief.[11] For Dr Robertson, the cause of Christiana's moral insanity was clear: she was a victim of hereditary madness, unable to escape the tragic medical history of her father, sister and brother. For Parry, this diagnosis and proof of a hereditary taint provided all the evidence he needed to present a plea of insanity to the court and, if accepted, save her from a guilty verdict.

While Parry worked on Christiana's case, he had also been retained to defend Reverend John Selby Watson, the only other person on trial for murder in the January session of the Old Bailey. On 8 October 1871, Watson had beaten his wife to death with the butt of a pistol at their home in Stockwell and hidden her body in a closet. Three days later, he penned a suicide note in which he confessed to his wife's murder and then unsuccessfully attempted to kill himself by taking prussic acid. The crime was every bit as complex and sensational as Christiana's and, on 10 January 1872, Parry submitted an application to the court to postpone her trial until the fate of the reverend had been decided. In court, Watson pleaded insanity and Parry provided an eloquent defence. He claimed that Watson experienced a temporary loss of sanity after having a difficult marriage and losing his job as the headmaster of Stockwell Grammar School, a post he had held for twenty-five years. The jury accepted these facts as provocation and found him guilty, though they also recommended mercy. Unfortunately, the judge disagreed with their recommendation and sentenced the reverend to death on 13 January 1872.

As the country debated the Watson verdict, the press geared up for the trial of Christiana Edmunds; one, they expected, would 'acquire a fascination and interest' not felt since the case of William Palmer in 1856, the notorious Rugeley poisoner.[12] On the morning of Monday, 15 January 1872, the wait was finally over and Christiana was taken from her cell in Newgate and led to the Old Bailey, the courthouse next door. Her trial took place in the Old Court, a room described by one writer as a 'mean place' in which 'a surgeon would be ashamed to cut off a leg'. The room was about forty-feet square, with the Judge's bench running along the north side and bearing the silver sword of justice in its centre. On the west were three windows to light the room under which lay the jury box below and, on the east, rows of benches for 'privileged spectators' and representatives of the press. Finally, on the south side, sat the prisoner's dock; a box with glass panels on two sides and open in the front, with a gallery above for members of the public.

The court room was so packed that its spectators struggled to catch a glimpse of Christiana, the now-infamous Chocolate Cream Killer, as she was escorted to the dock by a 'hard-faced' female warder and a male gaoler. Her entrance provided the press with another opportunity to scrutinise her appearance and to try and rectify this 'young, bright and not uncomely lady' with the 'horror of the crime charged against her' and the 'dread of the fate to which she stood exposed'.[13] Readers of the *Daily News* were treated to a complete analysis of Christiana's facial features by one of its writers, in a practice known as physiognomy. This highly popular pseudo-science judged a person's character from their facial characteristics. Physiognomists believed that the face was a window in to the soul and revealed the true extent of a person's sense of morality and integrity. That Christiana did not blush or tremble when placed in the dock not only heightened her allure to physiognomists but also made her character more difficult to gauge. The list of her crimes 'blanched the faces' of female spectators but Christiana, once again, remained calm and perfectly composed. This led the writer to suggest that Christiana might have once been a governess; a woman driven to patience and self-control after years of teaching under 'precarious condition'. This might, thought the writer, have also accounted for her rather 'careworn' and 'heard-featured' appearance. While he admitted that she looked no older than her mid-thirties, Christiana was fast approaching her forty-fourth birthday.

When it came to physical beauty, the *Daily News* portrayed Christiana as 'plain' with a rather dark complexion and a prominent forehead. But there was something about her lower features which truly fascinated:

The profile is irregular, but not unpleasing; the upper lip is long and convex; mouth slightly projecting; chin straight, long, and cruel; the lower jaw heavy, massive, and animal in its development. The lips are loose – almost pendulous – the lower one being fullest and projecting, and the mouth is exceptionally large. From the configuration of the lips the mouth might be thought weak, but at a glance the chin removes any such impression and Christiana Edmunds has a way of compressing the lips occasionally, when the left side of the mouth twists up with a sardonic, defiant determination, in which there is something of a weird comeliness.[14]

Christiana may not have been the most attractive criminal to grace the dock of the Old Bailey but she remained ladylike and elegant in her style and demeanour. She was dressed in a black velvet mantle, with a small fur tippet around her neck, black gloves and her hair smoothly braided into a chignon. After the clerk of the court read the indictment, Christiana pleaded 'not guilty' in a low but firm voice, prompting the proceedings to commence with the prosecution's opening statement.

The man leading the case against Christiana was William Ballantine, serjeant-at-law and great rival of Christiana's barrister, Serjeant Parry. Ballantine related the entire facts of the case to the court, beginning in September 1870 and ending in Christiana's arrest in August 1871. As at the hearing, the court then heard from a number of witnesses, including the family of Sidney Barker, Isaac Garrett, Caroline Stone, David Black, John Maynard and the boys who bought chocolate creams on Christiana's behalf. Throughout their evidence, Christiana remained calm and controlled as she wrote copious notes and followed each stage of the prosecution's case. It was only when Dr Beard was called to give evidence that her demeanour changed: 'her bosom heaved convulsively and her face flashed scarlet', wrote the *Daily News*. It took a few moments for Christiana to regain her composure and for her face go return to its state of 'leaden pallor'.[15] Her barrister had objected to the testimony of Dr Beard, believing that evidence from September 1870 was so remote that it bore no relevance to Christiana's charges. While the judge, Baron Martin, agreed with Parry, that much of his evidence was not relevant, he allowed the prosecution to question Dr Beard and to discuss the nature of his relationship with Christiana. Unfortunately, objections were raised before the public got a chance to hear any of the details:

> *Serjeant Ballantine*: Among your patients was the prisoner at the bar?
>
> *Dr Beard*: She was.
>
> *Ballantine*: Did she visit at your house?
>
> *Beard*: Certainly.
>
> *Ballantine*: And in consequence of something that occurred, did you make any sensation against her?
>
> *Serjeant Parry*: I object to this question, in this place, because it does not refer to the particular case we are trying.

Parry was, perhaps, trying to protect Christiana's sexual reputation by objecting to this question and, fortunately, it was upheld by the judge. When Ballantine withdrew the question, the case for the prosecution was brought to an end and the proceedings adjourned until the next day.[16]

When the trial resumed the next day, on the morning of Wednesday, 16 January, it was the turn of the defence to make its case to the court. In his opening statement, Serjeant Parry admitted the difficulties he had encountered in preparing his defence:

> *In my experience at the bar – which is now not a short experience – I never remember any case similar to this. In my reading of the criminal annals, both of this country and others, I never remember of a case*

similar to this, and I frankly own – I am not ashamed of it – that I
feel completely at a loss in my own mind how to place this case by way
of argument before you.

The problem was that Parry could not refute the evidence submitted
by the prosecution: that Christiana had purchased poison from Isaac
Garrett and used it to adulterate chocolate creams that she bought
from John Maynard which caused widespread illness across the town
and the tragic death of Sidney Barker. Nor could he deny the results
of the handwriting analysis which proved that Christiana had forged
letters to carry out her poisoning spree and had written the notes
inside the poisoned parcels. Above all, Parry struggled to understand
why Christiana had killed Sidney Barker, since she did not know the
boy and could therefore not have harboured towards him any feelings
of 'malice, hatred or dislike'. Accident or not, the evidence against
Christiana as the perpetrator of this murder was overwhelming. Parry
instead suggested to the court that Christiana was insane at the time
she committed her crimes and he had investigated her family history
in an attempt to prove his theory:

Insanity, you know, is an hereditary disease. It sometimes stops at one
generation, and revives at another; it sometimes goes directly down
from generation to generation. That her father and several of her
relatives were insane you won't have a doubt after the evidence I will
lay before you.

First to take the stand was Christiana's mother, Ann Edmunds, who
related the tragic tale of William's death in the asylum from general
paralysis of the insane. This testimony was so filled with sadness that
Christiana began to sob and cry bitterly. This was the first time she
had displayed any emotion in court and it continued as her mother
told the story of her brother, Arthur, and her sister, Louisa. To verify

Ann's story, Serjeant Parry called witnesses from Southall Park and Peckham House, who provided medical certificates relating to William Edmunds' confinement and death. He also called the proprietor of the Royal Earlswood to prove that Arthur died there in 1866 from epilepsy.

With her family history established, it was time to turn to its effects on her state of mind and Parry spoke first with Thomas Henry Cole, the chaplain at Lewes Prison. Cole had spoken frequently with Christiana from her arrival at Lewes in August 1871 until Christmas, when she was removed to Newgate. His testimony provided the first proof of her insanity:

> *I noticed a peculiar motion in her eyes and also in their formation the first time I saw her, and there was a vacant appearance in her face. Her conversation was perfectly coherent, but it struck me as very extraordinary, considering the position in which she was placed. I expected to find great excitement and dejection in a person charged with such an offence, instead of which I found she exhibited extraordinary levity, and when I conversed with her about her crime she burst into a life. I reasoned with her, but she seemed incapable of reasoning upon any grave matter. I frequently found her in tears and she would suddenly burst into laughter. I do not think she at all realised the position in which she was placed ... I am of the opinion, from all I observed of her, that the prisoner is of unsound mind.*

George and Alice Over, Christiana's former landlords, were the next witnesses to take the stand. They confirmed that a great change had come over Christiana after forming a friendship with Dr Beard. But Serjeant Parry would need more than the word of her friends to convince the jury that Christiana was insane and he proceeded to call, one by one, the medical men who had interviewed her in Newgate. They all agreed that Christiana was of unsound mind and severely lacking in any moral understanding but, on cross-examination,

Doctor Charles Lockhart Robertson, the physician appointed by the Court of Chancery, demonstrated a potential flaw in the insanity argument:

Serjeant Ballantine: Had she any moral sense?

Dr Charles Lockhart Robertson: To a certain degree she had.

Baron Martin: Do you mean that if she administered poison to another with intent to kill him she would not know she was doing wrong?

Robertson: I believe she would know that she was doing wrong if she committed an act.[17]

By admitting that Christiana knew the difference between the right and wrong, Dr Robertson had provided proof that she was not legally insane. Under the McNaughtan Rules, a defendant could successfully plead insanity only if she did not know the difference between right and wrong. After Dr Robertson, Dr Henry Maudsley expressed his belief in Christiana's moral insanity: 'I discovered an extreme deficiency of moral feeling with regard to the charge ... The prisoner exhibited extreme levity and laughed at the idea of her being executed for what she had done'.

Maudsley's testimony brought the case for the defence to a close. There had been a lot of talk of moral insanity and Serjeant Parry worried that the jury might not consider this evidence of legal insanity. In his summing up, he clarified the relationship between the two concepts: 'when a prisoner who had committed a great crime exhibited immediately before and immediately after it, and exhibited a hoity-toityness totally unbecoming her position, it was an indication of deficiency of morals, an indication that the mind was, to a certain extent, diseased'. Serjeant Parry also used this opportunity to remind the jury that Christiana's family was 'saturated with insanity'. But, in his closing remarks, the prosecution attacked the insanity defence with several valid points. First of all, Serjeant Ballantine attacked the notion of hereditary insanity by stating that it was a favourite defence among 'witnesses of this class' and that it was very much 'like saying that because a man's grandfather and grandmother had died of consumption his own lungs must be diseased and liable to give way upon the slightest pressure'. Furthermore, Dr Robertson's assertion that Christiana knew the difference between right and wrong had 'completely disposed' of the defence of insanity. If she knew that poisoning was wrong, said Ballantine, then she was guilty of the crime and had to be sentenced accordingly.[18]

In his address to the jury, the judge, Baron Martin, urged them to consider the following two questions: firstly, did Christiana give the poisoned creams to the boy, Adam May, to return to Maynard's for the purposes of selling on to others? If the answer is yes, the jury must deliver a guilty verdict. Secondly, did they believe that Christiana was in a state of mind as to be responsible for her actions? On this point the judge reminded the jury of Christiana's ingenious methods of carrying out her spree; from giving poisoned chocolates to random children in the street, to giving evidence against Maynard at the coroner's inquest and forging letters to destroy all trace of her transactions at Isaac Garrett's establishment. If they believed she was of sound mind, they must return a guilty verdict but if they found her to be insane, they could return a verdict of not guilty on the grounds of insanity.[19] The judge then dismissed the jury, leaving them with the monumental task of deciding the fate of Christiana Edmunds.

Chapter Eleven

"A Grievous Tale to Tell"

It took a little over one hour for the jury to agree on a verdict in the case of Christiana Edmunds. She appeared calm and unmoved as the foreman of the jury pronounced her guilty of the murder of Sidney Barker. Serjeant Parry's defence had failed and the room was now engulfed in a 'death-like stillness', as the realisation set in. Suddenly the silence was broken by the Clerk of Arraigns who asked Christiana if she knew of any reason why the death sentence should not be passed. With a sudden flush upon her pale cheeks, Christiana demanded that she be tried on the other charges, those relating to the poisoned parcels, so that her whole connection with the Beards might be revealed to the court. It was, she believed, 'owing to the treatment I have received from Dr Beard that I have been brought into this trouble'.[1] The judge, Baron Martin, listened attentively to Christiana and, while not disinclined to believe her, pointed out that no such evidence could affect the outcome of the trial. He then donned the black cap and sentenced Christiana to death.

This should have brought the proceedings to an end but Christiana had one final comment to make. When asked by the clerk if there was any reason why her execution might be stayed, Christiana declared that she was pregnant. This unexpected statement was made 'without any appearance of emotion and shame' and was the first time that a woman had 'plead the belly' since the case of Mary Ann Hunt in 1847. Whilst there was no real possibility of Christiana being pregnant (she had spent the last five months in police custody, after all), the court had to take her claim seriously. To do this, the court followed the customary practice of selecting a panel of matrons. There was no particular requirement or skill needed to act as a matron: the court simply selected twelve women from the public gallery who were then placed into the jury box and sworn in. The forewoman of the jury, again selected at random, then asked the court for the assistance of a surgeon. Fortunately, there were plenty of surgeons present in court that day but the first one to be suggested refused to assist. He was Nathaniel Paine Blaker, the man who had attended the Beard and Boys households after the delivery of the poisoned parcels, and who wished to have no further part in the Edmunds affair.[2] A sheriff then suggested James Beresford Ryley, a surgeon from the Woolwich division of the Metropolitan Police, who duly volunteered his service. From the Old Court, Christiana, Ryley and the matrons were escorted to a private room to begin the examination.

The purpose of the examination was to determine if Christiana was 'quick with child', or in a stage of pregnancy whereby the movement of the foetus could be felt. This was the only justifiable reason for postponing an execution. When the matrons had examined Mary Ann Hunt in 1847, they had unanimously agreed that she was not quick with child but she did, in fact, give birth to a healthy baby while awaiting her execution in Newgate. She faced the gallows for the financially-motivated murder of an elderly woman called Mary Stowell but being pregnant had saved her life: her death sentence was later commuted to transportation. As Dr Ryley looked over Christiana, he quickly realised that she was not quick with child but had plead the belly in a desperate attempt to avoid the 'dreadful doom of the gallows'. He asked her to retract her statement so that she might be spared the 'distress of a more minute scrutiny' but she persisted, forcing Ryley to examine her with a stethoscope.

Ryley, of course, found no evidence that Christiana was quick with child. This was little more than a ruse to save her life and an attempt to evoke sympathy for her ill-treatment at the hands of Dr Beard, the only man she had ever been romantically linked with. When Dr Ryley informed her of the result of his examination, the full peril of Christiana's situation dawned on her for the first time. Ryley would later write that 'awful aspect of her despair was very terrible to behold' and that the jury of matrons began to weep around her as she looked around the room in state of 'terrible woe'. With a weary agony in her voice, Christiana asked 'oh, how shall I sleep tonight?' to which Ryley advised her to ask the prison surgeon for a sedative. As they left the private room and returned to court, here ended 'one of the most solemn and pitiful scenes' in which Ryley had ever been an actor.[3]

Back in court, the jury of matrons returned its findings and the trial of Christiana Edmunds was formally concluded. She walked unaided from the bar and was escorted back to her cell in Newgate. Her cellmate, Eva Pierlo, was long gone, having served only three days for her charge of bigamy, and Christiana spent the rest of the day desperately persisting in her claim of pregnancy. When offered a second examination by the prison's surgeon, Christiana said 'it is of no use now' and refused to consent.[4] With the matter now dropped, she spent a final, lonely night in Newgate. The following morning, she departed London by train and headed to Lewes Prison, the place where her execution would soon take place. On the train, however, Christiana refused to accept that her destination was Lewes Prison. In her mind, she was going back to Brighton and this thought filled her with much contentment. When the train broke from the main line, indicating that her destination was Lewes, she became incredibly agitated and started to shout 'Dr Beard! Dr Beard! He has been the cause of this!' Christiana then opened the window and attempted to throw herself out of it. This sudden move prompted quick action from her escort who moved to bring her under his control. He warned Christiana that any similar action would result in her being restrained in handcuffs and this threat appeared to have some effect: Christiana calmed down but raved about Dr Beard for the remainder of the journey.[5]

While Christiana awaited the order for her execution, the press hotly debated the verdict of her trial. At one extreme was *Reynold's*, a popular Sunday newspaper, which called Christiana a 'monster of wickedness' and appeared very sceptical of her alleged insanity, as one writer commented: 'the method she displayed in attaining her object and the cunning evinced after condemnation in raising the false plea of pregnancy is far more suggestive of extreme shrewdness than of mental imbecility'.[6] Other newspapers shared a similar belief; that Christiana's efforts to hide her poisoning spree showed a 'consummate art, cunning and skill'[7] and made her appear bad, not mad. In expressing such views, however, these writers made the assumption that being insane would suddenly lessen Christiana's ability to solve problems and make decisions. Moreover, by universally condemning her as a cold–blooded killer, they also failed to consider her motivation for committing these crimes, as *The Era* pointed out. Writers of this weekly newspaper were extremely sympathetic towards Christiana, particularly in relation to her family's medical history. In one article, *The Era* admitted that 'a more awful tale of sorrow than the one wrung from the lips of her mother has never been heard and it makes one's heart bleed to repeat it'.[8] For the same reason, the *Illustrated Police News* declared that hanging Christiana would 'bring disgrace upon British justice'.[9]

The idea that executing a woman constituted a crime in itself was another sentiment which emerged among some newspapers of the national press. The gentleman's evening newspaper, the *Pall Mall Gazette*, was the first to voice this idea[10] and, in doing so, echoed a wider social concern about leading women to the gallows. In fact, over the course of the nineteenth century, there was a considerable decline in the prosecution of women for serious crimes, a larger decline in their conviction and a still larger decline in length of their prison sentences. The number of women executed dropped significantly too:[11] from 1861 to 1899, for example, only 28 of the 119 women sentenced to death were hanged for their crimes.[12] The only figure which rose for women in this period was the number who, like Christiana, plead insanity. Women were twice as likely as men to be acquitted on the grounds of insanity for similar crimes, a figure which increased from seven per cent of acquittals at the beginning of the Victorian period to seventeen per cent by the 1890s.[13] It was the redefinition of women from bad to mad that accounted for such changes in their legal treatment. Society found it easier to view female criminals as insane because it complemented Victorian gender ideology which characterised women as sensitive and delicate creatures, prone to bouts of hysteria and weak-mindedness.

Sympathy for Christiana's case extended beyond the national press too. In her home town of Margate, a number of clergymen, magistrates and people of influence drafted a petition to Queen Victoria for a royal pardon on 22 January. A similar petition was also created by the people of the city of Manchester, who cited 'various reasons' and the 'special circumstances of the case' as evidence of the need for royal clemency. Even the people of Brighton, who had once been horrified by Christiana and her crimes, re-evaluated their position. Led by Charles Lamb, the man who had unsuccessfully defended Christiana at her hearing, the petition for a commutation of the death sentence was signed by ex-Mayor of Brighton, a number of magistrates and 'many other gentlemen' of the town. Surprisingly, the petition was also signed by two of Christiana's victims: Elizabeth Boys and Isaac Garrett.[14]

Public petitions to Queen Victoria were accompanied by action from the medical men who had interviewed Christiana in Newgate. On January 19, William Wood, the physician from St Luke's Hospital, wrote a letter to the *Pall Mall Gazette* in which he reiterated his beliefs in her insanity:

I don't think any person in court who witnessed the almost childlike curiosity with which she walked forward to the front of the dock to hear the decision of the jury, and the absolute indifference with which in that awful moment she heard the dreaded sentence ... could doubt that her mind was incapable of estimating the difference between right and wrong as other persons do.[15]

Wood and his colleagues sent a certificate confirming Christiana's diagnosis of insanity to the Home Secretary, Henry Austin Bruce, in the hope of securing a reprieve. Around the same time, Bruce received a letter from Baron Martin, the judge who had condemned Christiana to death, in which he expressed his concerns about her impending execution. This was a significant about-turn for the man who had criticised her defence in court, claiming that an insanity plea was routinely abused by 'people of means' in an attempt to evade the gallows.[16] Perhaps the judge had developed a view similar to that of the eminent toxicologist, Alfred Swaine Taylor, who provided a logical and almost-scientific view of her case:

In some trials there has been a tendency to rely upon hereditary predisposition as almost the sole proof of insanity in the criminal. In the case of Christiana Edmunds, convicted of the crime of poisoning on an extensive scale, no evidence of intellectual insanity or of homicidal impulse could be found. There was a motive, an endeavour to fix the crime upon others, great skill in its perpetration, concealment with a full knowledge of the consequences of the act and an endeavour to avoid the punishment by a false plea of pregnancy. In short, the conduct of the woman throughout was that of a sane criminal. The jury found her guilty; but in consequence of proof being furnished that many members of her family had suffered under insanity in some form, it was supposed that there might be some latent degree of insanity in her case, not discoverable by the ordinary methods of examination.[17]

Whatever the reason for his change of heart, the judge's recommendation was the first stage in the Victorian appeals process and his word prompted a re-investigation of the verdict. The Home

Secretary then appointed two physicians to decide if Christiana really was insane. The first man appointed was Sir William Gull, an Essex-born physician, who had graduated MB from London University with honours in physiology, comparative anatomy and surgery. He received his MD in 1848 and had a thriving private practice alongside numerous official appointments, including consulting physician at Guy's Hospital. He came to public attention in 1871 when he attended the Prince of Wales during a severe illness with typhoid fever and he was knighted in the same month as Christiana stood trial at the Old Bailey. As well-respected and knowledgeable as Gull was, he had very little experience in mental health, having worked only briefly on a lunatic ward at Guy's in 1843, and the public naturally expressed some concerns over his appointment by the Home Secretary.

It was hoped, however, that the other man appointed to interview Christiana might make up for any of Gull's shortcomings. His name was Dr William Orange and he was the medical superintendent of Broadmoor, the state asylum for the criminally insane. Orange was born in Torquay in 1833 and was the son of an independent preacher. He had trained to be a doctor at St Thomas' Hospital in London and, after qualifying, had travelled the Continent extensively while in charge of a patient. On his return to England, he took the post of assistant medical officer at the Surrey County Lunatic Asylum, leaving to go to Broadmoor in 1863, the year it opened. Orange and Gull visited Christiana in Lewes Prison on 23 January 1872, believing that 'personal communication' would be the most satisfactory method of determining her state of mind. There are no surviving minutes of their conversation but Gull drew up a letter to the Home Secretary in which he recorded his and Dr Orange's thoughts about Christiana. In the letter, Gull states that they talked first with Christiana about her childhood, a period they called 'tranquil, easy and indifferent', before moving to discuss her adult life. She told them about her father's death in the asylum, her brother being 'idiotic and epileptic' and Louisa's repeated bouts of hysteria. She also talked of her arrival in Brighton and subsequent meeting with the Beards. From her account, they concluded that Christiana had suffered from 'mental perversion' and 'defective memory' for the last three years, a date which roughly corresponds with Christiana falling in love with Dr Beard and the beginning of her plot to kill his wife.

On the subject of her crimes, Orange and Gull harboured no doubts about Christiana's guilt and their examination pointed to her 'weak and disordered intellect' and 'confused and perverted feelings' as the cause of her criminality. At no point did Christiana deny any of the charges against her; she admitted to the purchasing and distribution of poison but she seemed incapable, wrote Gull, of realising that she had committed murder. She, in fact, tried to justify her conduct but Gull provided no examples of her argument, stating only that her reasoning was 'insane'. After this long conversation, they concluded that Christiana was of 'unsound mind' and they required no further evidence to prove it. Gull's final statement, that Christiana 'ought to be treated accordingly', hinted at a reprieve from the death penalty but she would have to wait for a final decision from the Home Secretary before her fate was made clear.

Two days later, on 25 January 1872, the news Christiana had been waiting for was finally announced: Home Secretary Bruce had accepted the results of Orange and Gull's interview and declared Christiana insane. Her death sentence would not be carried out and she would instead be sent to Broadmoor Asylum. Christiana's response to this decision was not recorded but she likely felt much relief at escaping the gallows. For many of the national newspapers, however, the decision constituted a gross 'miscarriage of justice' that flew in the face of trial by jury, a British institution.[18] As *Reynold's* argued, the jury had found Christiana guilty, despite claims of insanity from several esteemed psychiatrists. It was therefore felt that Home Secretary Bruce's decision impeded the law from running its natural course.[19]

This left many people feeling that Christiana had been reprieved as a result of her privileged background and social status, not because she was truly insane at the time she poisoned. The *Spectator* was the first to air this sentiment, claiming that Christiana would have faced the gallows had she been a 'poor woman' instead of a 'lady of refinement'.[20] Some newspapers took this one step further by arguing that a stay in Broadmoor was an easy punishment: 'And the guilty woman [Christiana] was exempted from all penalty but that of living sane among the mad ... in theory only equal to life in a nun's cell'. The problem with such a punishment, the writer argued, was that it gave people of means the impression that they could get away with murder.[21]

While it is true that Christiana was the first woman to have her death sentence commuted to incarceration in Broadmoor, this decision was not the result of any special treatment. In reality, her case highlighted the problematic definition of legal insanity and the often-difficult relationship between medicine and the law. That Christiana was not insane in the legal sense of the word could not be contested: she knew that it was wrong to purchase poison under a false name and then disseminate it around Brighton. The problem was that she possessed no understanding of the moral consequences of her actions, a fact confirmed by numerous physicians but one without legal basis or precedent. Coupled with her family's history of insanity, the authorities began to feel very uneasy about the strength of her conviction. The *Daily News* considered Christiana's reprieve a necessary move in the face of 'haphazard' and 'unsatisfactory' methods of diagnosing insanity[22] when, in reality, it was the first time that the authorities – both medical and legal – had dealt with such a scenario.

But whatever the public thought about Christiana and her mind, they could not undo the Home Secretary's decision. In Brighton, the news of her respite was met with indignation from the town's mayor, James Cordy Burrows. The town had paid a substantial amount to prosecute

Christiana: for the six-monthly period ending in December 1871, Brighton had spent over £998 on criminal prosecutions, a figure which included her hearing but not the cost of her trial at the Old Bailey or her examination in Newgate by Sir Gull and Dr Orange. To make matters worse, the Home Secretary now demanded that Brighton meet the weekly cost of Christiana's care in Broadmoor, a fee which amounted to fourteen shillings per week. This was an unusual decision, considering that Christiana's family were in a position to pay the cost themselves and had made this clear to the Home Secretary. The man who had stepped up financially was Christiana's brother-in-law, Sydney Cornish Harrington, whose sister, Georgiana, had married William Edmunds before he emigrated to South Africa in 1854. By the time of Christiana's trial, Sydney was a retired army captain, living in relative luxury with his family in Datchworth in Hertfordshire. Despite their familial connection, Harrington had never met Christiana before she shot to fame and notoriety as the Chocolate Cream Killer but he contributed to the cost of her defence and met with her in Lewes Prison and, later, in Newgate. These meetings had prompted Sydney to write to the Home Secretary to ask that Christiana's death sentence be commuted. His letter provides a rare glimpse into Christiana's state of mind at the end of 1871 and his observations led him to the conclusion that she was the most insane person he had ever met. Harrington was struck first by Christiana's appearance: her pupils were dilated, her eyes had an unnatural glare and she had a 'semblance of looking to space, however interested she might be in the conversation'. Harrington commented on the 'utter impossibility of confining her to any particular subject of conversation'. Every sentence she spoke mentioned Dr Beard and she repeated over and over how she was going to Brighton to see him. In between these chants, she claimed to be a victim of conspiracy and told Harrington that 'the Police have sent a woman to break me and she has been following me all night'. This was followed by further chants of 'I am going to see Dr Beard! I am going to Brighton!' At the end of the meeting, Harrington asked the governor if he might shake Christiana's hand. The governor consented and Harrington asked: 'Chrissie, won't you shake hands with me?' She replied 'oh yes' but had barely touched his hand when she began to chant about Dr Beard and Brighton all over again.

In his letter, Harrington confirmed the family's history of madness, beginning with the death of William Edmunds in Peckham House in 1847. He also provides an interesting anecdote about the younger William Edmunds who he claimed had threatened suicide if he could not have Georgiana's hand in marriage. This dramatic threat so terrified both families that permission was immediately granted and William married Georgiana a few weeks later. Whether his threat was genuine or not, this convinced Harrington of the family's taint of insanity and had contributed to his belief that Christiana needed care and cure, not a death sentence.[23]

Despite Harrington's offer to pay for his sister-in-law's care in Broadmoor, the Home Secretary was adamant that financial responsibility lay with the town of Brighton. As the mayor argued, this decision meant that town's rate-payers would be 'saddled as long as Miss Edmunds lives' and it was, in his opinion, 'the grossest piece of injustice ever perpetrated'.[24] Burrows was as stubborn as Home Secretary Bruce: he blocked every move made by the town clerk and coroner, David Black, to collect the money for Christiana's board and repeated his complaints of injustice at every opportunity. Even the threat of legal action by the Treasury would not convince him to comply. The matter did eventually go to court but Burrows had one last card to play: he claimed that the financial burden lay with the city of Canterbury, Christiana's parish of residence, and not with Brighton, the parish of 'irremovability'. The judge was suitably convinced and, in 1875, Canterbury was billed over £56 in expenses and ordered to pay the 14s per week until the time of Christiana's death.[25]

On 27 June 1872, Christiana received her formal respite from the government and the warrant authorising her immediate removal to Broadmoor Asylum for the Criminally Insane. She was to be confined until the 'signification of Her Majesty's pleasure' and to be accompanied by a document certifying her state of mind.[26] This was completed by Richard Turner, the prison's surgeon, whose observations make for interesting reading. Turner was not at all convinced by Sir Gull and Dr Orange's diagnosis of insanity, nor of the need to confine Christiana in an asylum. On her certificate, he made his thoughts as clear as possible: 'after 10 months daily supervision, I fail to satisfy myself that Christiana Edmunds is insane or irresponsible for her actions'. He added that 'she has never shown symptoms of being suicidal or dangerous to others' and 'has manifested no delusion in my presence'. He did, however, admit that 'she is of delicate constitution and disposed to be hysterical' but he provided no examples of her conduct while incarcerated at Lewes. He also noted that she was 'much weakened by her long detention in prison'[27] but it is unclear if Turner was referring to Christiana's mental or physical health, or perhaps a combination of both. Whatever her weaknesses, Christiana arrived at Broadmoor Asylum on 5 July determined to look her best. She was wearing 'a large amount of false hair', false teeth and had painted her cheeks with rouge; the Venus of Broadmoor had finally arrived.

Chapter Twelve

"The Venus of Broadmoor"

The Broadmoor Criminal Lunatic Asylum was set amongst acres of pine trees in the tranquil and picturesque Windsor Forest in the county of Berkshire. In 1865, a visitor to the site remarked on its 'lofty and handsome' buildings, claiming that a 'warmer and more comfortable-looking structure had never been erected in a more wild, though beautiful, situation'. Behind its high walls, the visitor found a female croquet party on the lawn and a group of men in the garden playing bagatelle. Inside, he found the patients were treated 'with an almost excess of care' and enjoyed all the freedoms and pleasures of ordinary people: 'they can see their friends, write to whom they please' and 'can take what exercise they like in the spacious airing grounds'. But there was one crucial difference between the patients at Broadmoor and ordinary lunatics: 'they can, in short, do anything but pass the boundaries which shut them in forever from the world beyond. Within these they live and die'.[1]

When Broadmoor opened in May 1863, the long-standing question of where to house England's criminal lunatics was finally answered. In previous decades, the provision for criminal lunatics was haphazard and inadequate. The Bethlem Hospital in London had opened two wings for the detention of the criminally insane in 1816 but, beyond this, such patients were housed in ordinary asylums or prisons. That the criminally insane were perceived as dangerous and in need of a permanent place of confinement helped to bring the problem to the attention of the government. According to the Select Committee of House of Commons of 1860:

*To mix such persons, that is criminal lunatics, with other patients
is a serious evil; it is detrimental to the other patients as well as to
themselves; but to liberate them on recovery, as a matter of course, is a
still greater evil, and could not be sanctioned, for the danger to society
would be extreme and imminent.*[2]

In the same year, the government passed the Criminal Lunatic Asylum
Act which authorised the creation of Broadmoor and gave the Home
Secretary control over its management and the admission of patients.
It took less than three years for Broadmoor to be constructed and,
on 23 May 1863, it welcomed its first patients, a group of women
transferred from the Bethlem Hospital. Nine months later, the women
were joined by the first intake of male patients and, by the end of 1864,
the population of Broadmoor had risen to 200 men and 100 women.[3]

Tasked with the supervision and cure of these criminal lunatics was Dr
John Meyer, Broadmoor's first superintendent. Meyer was well-suited to
this new and challenging post, having gained a considerable amount of
experience with the mentally ill. Between 1844 and 1854, he worked as
the supervisor to the Convict Lunatic Asylum in Tasmania and as chief
resident physician of the Surrey County Asylum from 1858 to 1862.
Meyer had military experience too; he managed the Civil Hospital in
Smyrna during the Crimean War, which perhaps accounts for his tough
attitude towards Broadmoor's more dangerous criminals. For this group,
he advocated the use of cages for periods of solitary confinement, a move
which contravened the principles of moral treatment, the asylum's guiding
philosophy. When Meyer died in May 1870, his deputy, and the man who
had declared Christiana insane, William Orange, became Broadmoor's
new superintendent. He removed Meyer's cages and steered the asylum
in a more humanitarian direction, during which time Broadmoor and its
residents enjoyed a period of relative peace and prosperity.

Orange was in his second year as superintendent when Christiana
arrived at Broadmoor and she was, in many ways, a unique patient.

She was not the only woman detained after committing murder: in fact, forty per cent of the women at Broadmoor were murderesses,[4] but Christiana's choice of victim made her stand out among the others. This was because Victorian women were far more likely to murder members of their own household than a stranger or other persons outside of the domestic sphere.[5] The overwhelming majority of Broadmoor's murderesses had killed or attempted to kill their own children: between 1863 and 1902, 286 women were confined as a result of committing this crime. Unlike Christiana, however, most of these women were married and belonged to the working or lower middle classes where socio-economic problems, like financial difficulties and a lack of domestic help, contributed to a mother's mental breakdown.[6] One such woman was Margaret Jones, a 31-year-old housewife from Warrington, who arrived at Broadmoor in September 1872, two months after Christiana. Margaret had murdered her two daughters earlier that year by drowning them in a large tub and was found insane during her committal hearing. Margaret's life was characterised by isolation and deprivation: she was frequently alone as her husband worked long hours, money was tight and she had no family nearby. To exacerbate these problems, she had lost two sons in infancy from natural causes. However inexcusable her crime, Margaret's life had been a difficult one and she was typical of many of the women who found themselves confined in Broadmoor.[7]

Christiana, then, faced none of the social and economic problems that plagued the lives of many of her fellow patients. She was a very different sort of patient but Dr Orange was proven right in his assertions of her moral insanity shortly after her arrival. In an entry from her file, dated 17 August 1872, he admitted that his findings from her interview in Newgate had been 'fully confirmed by her conduct and conversation since admission.' While she was 'quiet and orderly' in her behaviour and did not pose any physical threat to herself of others, she expressed no remorse for her crimes nor offered any explanation regarding the motive. When her mother came to visit a few days later, she told Dr Orange that Christiana had never expressed sorrow, not even for the 'trouble' she had caused her family. But the purpose of Ann's visit to Broadmoor was not just to see Christiana. She had bad news: Christiana's brother, William, had passed away in South Africa, at the age of 43. When William had left England in 1854 to start a new life, he had gone to Grahamstown, a city in the Eastern Cape province. Over the next eight years, he worked as a medical officer at the Albany Hospital and as a surgeon to the Grahamstown Volunteers and the Katberg Convict Station. In June 1862 he left Grahamstown for his most challenging role, having been appointed the new superintendent of the asylum on Robben Island, an institution in desperate need of reform. William was an avid supporter of moral treatment who followed the methods of John Conolly to the letter: he hired more staff, increased their wages, abolished unnecessary instances of mechanical restraint, improved the patients' diet and provided opportunities for leisure.[8] In short, he transformed the asylum and the lives of its patients and he was, perhaps, inspired and motivated by the experiences of his father in Peckham House thirty years earlier.

Ann Edmunds told Dr Orange that her son had experienced some mental health issues before his death in 1872 but this cannot be verified by any sources. On the same day she also told Dr Orange that Christiana was not truthful as a child and, maybe, this was her attempt to demonstrate the extent of insanity in her family. For Christiana, the news of his death prompted barely any reaction, as Dr Orange observed: 'she appeared quite unable to experience any feeling of sorrow, although she tried to look grieved'.[9] The sad reality of William's death is that it left Christiana with only one surviving sibling, Mary, who wrote to her frequently over the coming years.

Like other asylums, Broadmoor actively encouraged its patients to maintain contact with family and friends. Letters to and from patients flowed freely, though they were subject to inspection by asylum staff.

The correspondence between Christiana and Mary reads like the typical sisterly conversation of teenagers, focusing almost exclusively on make-up and clothing. This is hardly surprising as Christiana's vanity and desire to be attractive had been noted on several occasions by Dr Orange. On 2 November 1872, asylum staff inspected one of Christiana's letter to Mary and found that inside the envelope, she had 'ingeniously fastened' a single scrap of paper, covered in extremely small writing. In this communication, Christiana asked her sister to bring some clandestine 'articles of wearing apparel' and half a crown to give to one of the attendants, presumably as a bribe. When presented with the scrap of paper, Christiana 'exhibited neither surprise nor shame' and this behaviour continued unabated. Her letters to Mary in the following year focus on methods of applying paint to the face and hatching schemes to procure articles of clothing that made her look different from the other patients. Clearly, Christiana had no love for Broadmoor's uniform. Over the course of 1874, more and more parcels from Mary arrived, each one inventively hidden with another beauty item or pieces of false hair. Christiana's smuggling became an increasing source of frustration for Broadmoor's matron, Mrs Jackson. In June 1874, Mary sent a leather cushion to her sister but Mrs Jackson refused to hand it over. In a letter to Dr Orange, she stated that the cushion was 'not really sent in to amuse or please' but was, in fact, 'a deceptive manner of conveying false hair. She has already great quantities which have been obtained by deception'.[10] Ironically, Broadmoor would have allowed Christiana to have the false hair, had she gone through the proper channels. By smuggling it in, it reflected a much more serious problem: that Christiana was driven by a need to be deceitful.

Her love of deception turned into a 'mania' over the remainder of 1874 and 1875. Christiana turned her attentions from Dr Beard to Reverend Henry Cole, the chaplain of Lewes Prison. In July it was discovered that Christiana had sent letters to Cole through her sister,

Mary. Given her efforts to conceal the correspondence from the staff at Broadmoor, it is likely that the letters were of an amorous nature and they demonstrate her need to be the centre of other people's attention. In her file, Dr Orange wrote that he would have 'no objection' to Christiana writing to the chaplain but, once again, it was 'in conformity with her state of mind to prefer mystery and concealment'. Letters to an attendant were found in her room in the following April but there are no surviving details of their contents. During the same search, the matron found that 'numerous articles' had been secreted and Christiana was forced to change rooms. Two months later, another search of her room found additional hidden items amongst the furniture. As she sought to conceal these things, it was noted that her mind became more 'impaired' and her conduct increasingly 'irrational'. Dr Orange was at a loss to understand her behaviour: 'she deceives for the pure love of deception and with no sufficient motive'.

As Christiana became more irrational, her behaviour became increasingly difficult to manage. While in ward three of her block, 'her delight and amusement seemed to be in practicing the art of ingeniously tormenting several of the more irritable patients'. The purpose of her torment was 'to complain of their language to her' and to evoke sympathy for her situation. Likewise, when her mother came to visit, she omitted her make-up, shed false tears and complained of the 'injustice and cruelty' with which she was treated. Of course, her treatment at Broadmoor was far from cruel but Christiana was a woman who needed to be the centre of attention and, when she was not, she would go to extreme lengths to get it. Once again, she had demonstrated that she was 'unable to resist the desire to conceal' and be deceitful, even when there was no call for it.

This behaviour resulted in Christiana being moved to another ward in July 1876. The move had a positive effect, she became 'tolerably tranquil and orderly in her behaviour'[11] and finally settled into the routine of life in Broadmoor. By this time, Christiana was one of 125 female patients, split over two self-contained blocks and completely separate from the male section of the asylum. Her day began at 6.00 am (or 7.00 am during the winter), she rose for prayers led by the chaplain and ate a breakfast of bread and butter, served with tea. For most patients at Boradmoor, the day was then spent at work, one of the foundations of moral treatment, and Christiana may have worked as a seamstress, in the laundry or, perhaps, tending to the garden. The asylum was virtually self-sufficient: every item of clothing was made in-house and much of the patient's food came from its farm or garden.

Between work and meals, Dr Orange encouraged his patients to pursue their personal interests, another defining principle of moral treatment. For Christiana, this included embroidery, sewing and painting. She also copied pictures, a hobby which had brought her closer to Dr Beard some ten years earlier. Brighton might have felt like a million miles away but, generally, her life was still as comfortable and fulfilling as it had once been. She had the freedom to spend time outside, either playing games like croquet or simply walking in the airing court attached to her block. Good behaviour was also rewarded with a ride in the carriage or an accompanied stroll around the local area. Over the years, Broadmoor also developed its own evening entertainment, a varied programme with music, dances and amateur dramatics.[12] Life at Broadmoor was highly-regulated but, overall, it provided its patients with a good standard of living, regardless of how much Christiana complained.

Despite an overall improvement in her behaviour in 1877 and 1878, she continued to display excessive levels of vanity and frivolity. She painted her face each morning, worked hard to achieve a 'youthful appearance' and dressed herself as best she could for inspections. Her conversation and manner demonstrated to Dr Orange that she harboured 'sexual and amatory ideas'[13] and she was, perhaps, guilty of flirting with male members of staff whenever the opportunity arose. If her thoughts returned to Dr Beard, then there is no mention of it in her file, but she was never able to appreciate the severity of her crimes in Brighton and how it related to her confinement in Broadmoor. Nevertheless, in October 1880, Christiana penned a letter to the Home Office in which she eloquently petitioned for her release:

Sir, I venture to petition for my release from the Broadmoor Asylum. I have been eight years in confinement and am very anxious to regain my liberty. I earnestly trust that my conduct has been such as to gain me the favourable regard of the Superintendent and those over me. I shall feel very grateful if you will kindly consider my petition and grant my release.

I remain Sir, Your Humble Petitioner,
Christiana Edmunds.

This appeal was accompanied by a letter from Broadmoor which stated that Christiana was 'tranquil and orderly in her conduct' but that her mind remained 'unsound'. [14] Many years had passed since Christiana was a free woman however, and the British political landscape had changed significantly. Henry Austin Bruce was no longer the Home Secretary, after the Liberals were defeated by the Conservatives in 1874. Bruce had since been raised to the peerage and was now known as Lord Aberdare, and busied himself with his presidency of the Royal Historical Society. In 1880 the Home Secretary was Richard Assheton Cross, a man not well acquainted with the details of Christiana's case but who rejected her appeal on 4 November. This is hardly surprising given her status as a patient detained at Her Majesty's pleasure and who had shown no remorse for her crimes nor improvement in her mental state, despite extensive moral treatment. Christiana did not appeal again but, in 1884, Dr Orange noted that all of the paperwork authorising her confinement had been lost but he did not push the government to reproduce it nor did it effectuate her release.

Two years later, in 1886, Dr Orange retired from Broadmoor and Dr David Nicolson became the new superintendent. Nicolson had worked in several convict prisons and had published a series of articles entitled *The Morbid Psychology of the Criminal*. He had much experience to offer and was every bit as caring as Dr Orange, though more organised in his approach to running and managing the asylum. Nicholson found Christiana to be a 'quiet and orderly' patient, 'cheerful and pleasant in conversation' but 'very vain'. He wrote in her file that she 'courts and desires attention and notoriety' and 'pushes herself forward on all occasions'. This may have been Christiana's attempt at gaining recognition and attention from her new superintendent but, for Nicolson, it was further proof of her insanity. A few years later, he reported that she was 'always ready to be taken notice of and to endeavour to place herself in the foreground of whatever is going in'. Even at the age of 62, Christiana's desire to be the centre of attention had not decreased in the slightest.

Dr Nicholson made few notes on Christiana in his ten years as the superintendent of Broadmoor. When he retired in 1895, Dr Richard Brayn assumed control and he employed very different methods to his two predecessors. Brayn had worked as the medical governor of the Woking and Aylesbury prisons and believed in discipline and using punishments like solitary confinement. He did, however, revamp the asylum internally which gave it an airy and cheerful feel, in spite of his strict regime.[15] At the time of his arrival, Christiana was in her mid-sixties and entering a period of ill-health. She suffered bouts of influenza in 1897 and 1900, the latter of which was 'rather severe' and left her weak and looking more aged. In the following year, she had catarrh, chronic constipation and dyspepsia but made significant improvement after taking regular doses of cascara sagrada, a natural laxative. But this recovery was short-lived: by the end of 1901, her sight began to fail rapidly and she complained of 'vague pains' about the body, particularly in her upper back. She was advised not to attend the New Years' Ball but Christiana could not miss being the centre of attention, even during a period of illness.

As her physical health declined, she became 'gloomy' and 'dissatisfied' and argued frequently with other patients. By 1906, she was unable to walk without assistance, suffered bouts of neuralgia and had to be removed to the infirmary in November. But even in this state, her vanity was 'unabated' and she continued to worry about her personal appearance. While in the infirmary one afternoon, Dr Brayn overhead the following conversation between Christiana and a patient who had come to visit her:

Christiana: How am I looking?

Patient: Fairly well.

Christiana: I think I am improving, I hope I shall be better in a fortnight, if so, I shall astonish them; I shall get up and dance! I was a Venus before and I shall be a Venus again!

But the Venus of Broadmoor would not get up and dance again. Over the next year, she became weaker and experienced pains in her legs that made her spend most of her time in bed, only getting up on the occasional afternoon. In April 1907, Dr Brayn observed that she talked a great deal to herself and complained of being left outside in the airing court for an entire night when she had, in fact, been bedridden for over a month. Her condition continued to weaken and she died of 'senile debility', a Victorian term for old age, on the morning of 19 September 1907.[16]

Though it had been almost forty years since the Case of the Chocolate Cream Killer hit the headlines, Christiana's passing did not go unnoticed by the press. One newspaper called her crimes a 'curiously cunning and subtle attempt at wholesale poisoning' and her trial one of the 'most notorious of the last century'.[17] Others recalled this 'long-forgotten tragedy' as they related the facts of the case to the Edwardian public.[18] Christiana was still remembered as late as 1970 when ITV dramatised the play, *Christiana Edmunds*, which explored her crimes in depth and prompted the nation to think twice about taking chocolates from strangers. Christiana's cultural reputation has therefore endured long after her death: she was Brighton's lady poisoner, a woman driven mad by sexual desire and vanity, and her celebrity status in England's criminal history is something she would likely be proud of.

Epilogue

I n 2013 the former Broadmoor psychiatrist, Professor Tony Maden, reviewed the case of Christiana Edmunds and suggested that she was suffering from Narcissistic Personality Disorder at the time she committed her crimes.[19] This disorder was not discovered until several decades after Christiana's death but its clinical presentation bears a striking resemblance to her behaviour during the early 1870s. At its core, Narcissistic Personality Disorder creates an individual who displays an unrealistic sense of superiority and who possesses an overwhelming need for attention, affection and admiration. When these needs are not met, the individual will resort to any number of manipulative tactics to restore their personal sense of power and prestige. Because the individual is driven by their own sense of narcissistic entitlement, these manipulative tactics can take any form, from the destruction of a perceived rival to homicidal violence, and are not accompanied by feelings of remorse or empathy towards those around them.[20] In this understanding, then, Christiana's poisoning spree was an uncontrollable reaction to the loss of Dr Beard's attention and affection which threatened her sense of entitlement and inflated sense of self. Feeling genuinely slighted, she came to view Emily Beard as implicit in this loss of Dr Beard's affections and therefore felt justified in trying to take her life. As for her other victims, they were simply an attempt at gaining greater glory in a scheme which played to her sense of grandiosity.

Underneath the narcissist's distorted sense of self-worth, there are much darker emotions at play. There is a constant and 'pervasive sense of deprivation' and a number 'seemingly insatiable inner needs' which continually attack the self-esteem and cause feelings of worthlessness and depressive moods.[21] This explains why Christiana continued in her quest for Dr Beard's affections, even though it made her feel uncomfortable and like she was going mad: it was a compulsion that she could not escape. Similarly, in prison and at Broadmoor, she could never fully settle into the routine of life because she was treated like everyone else and not given the special status that she believed was her rightful entitlement.

Whatever the truth about her motivations, her death brought the story of the Edmunds family full circle: beginning with her father in Peckham House in 1847 and ending with her own demise in Broadmoor six decades later. The Victorian asylum had come to symbolise and unite the Edmunds, a family plagued by bereavement and mental illness and scarred by the effects of syphilis. If Christiana really was a victim of Narcissistic Personality Disorder, these experiences, combined with a genetic predisposition perhaps inherited from her mother's family, may well have contributed to its onset in her adult life.[22] Whatever prompted Christiana to commit mass poisoning, her obsession with Dr Beard had brought the town of Brighton to its knees in the summer of 1871. It resulted in the tragic death of a 4-year-old boy and, perhaps, in the deaths of many more who sadly passed unnoticed by the authorities, though the records which might confirm this have sadly not survived. In the aftermath of her poisoning spree, the town of Brighton made a full recovery and regained its position as Victorian England's favourite seaside destination but not everyone in Christiana's story fared so well. For Dr Charles Beard, the man at the centre of the case, the events of the early 1870s would have a long-lasting impact. In 1886, he was admitted to St Andrews asylum in Northamptonshire after suffering from mental illness for the last fifteen years, a date which corresponds to Christiana's poisoning spree. According to his medical certificates, Beard believed himself to be the victim of a conspiracy, brought on by a large number of deaths after vaccinations administered some years earlier. He told asylum staff that another Brighton doctor had made claims of bestiality against him and, later, he was accused of taking bribes. Beard believed that this conspiracy against him included the town's police, post office and a number of highly-respected citizens. Staff at the asylum found him to be a 'courteous, affable and highly intelligent' man who conversed 'freely and rationally' on the events of his life, including his time as a General Practitioner and Local Government Board inspector. Interestingly, he did not divulge a single detail about Christiana and her poisoning spree.

Dr Beard's belief in the conspiracy heightened in the years after his admission and, in 1889, he claimed to have witnessed an attack on another patient by five attendants. The Commissioners in Lunacy suggested that Beard be transferred, first to an unnamed asylum and later to the Holloway Sanatorium in London. He was never discharged and died there in 1916, at the age of 88.[23] With her husband in the asylum, Emily Beard left Brighton and headed to London. She lived first with her daughter and grandson in Lupus Street before moving in with her son, Hugh, and his family. By 1911 the effects of old age had set in: she was described in the census as 'feeble-minded' and died the following year at the age of 84.

Christiana outlived the two remaining members of her own family. After her daughter's confinement in Broadmoor, Ann Edmunds left Brighton and died in Steyning in Sussex in 1893. Christiana's sister, Mary, died five years later, in 1898, and was survived by her husband, Edward Foreman. There is no mention of Christiana's reaction to these events in her notes from Broadmoor: she is described as 'silly and frivolous' in the year of Mary's death and 'quiet and orderly' around the time of her mother's passing.[24] Like the severity of her crimes, she remained unable to appreciate the consequences of these major events and instead retreated into a world where nothing outside of her invented selves, the Dorothea and the Venus, truly mattered.

Notes

15 March 1847

1. Quoted in G. Davis, 'The Most Deadly Disease of Asylumdom: General Paralysis of the Insane and Scottish Psychiatry, c. 1840–1890, *Journal of the Royal College of Physicians Edinburgh*, *vol.* 42, no.3, http://www.rcpe.ac.uk/sites/default/files/davis.pdf, 2012, p.267.
2. E. R. Wallace & J. Gach (eds.), *History of Psychiatry and Medical Psychology*, New York, Springer Science and Business Media, 2008, p.391.
3. J. C. Prichard, *A Treatise on Insanity and Other Disorders of the Mind*, Philadelphia, Carey & Hart, 1837, p.100.
4. *Ibid*, p.103.
5. *Ibid*, p.104.
6. *Ibid*, p.105.
7. F. Haslam, *From Hogarth to Rowlandson: Medicine in Art in Eighteenth-Century Britain*, Liverpool, Liverpool University Press, 1996, p.157.
8. *Ibid*, J. Wallis, 'This Fascinating and Fatal Disease', *The Psychologist*, *vol* 5, no.10, 2012, p.790.
9. B. Forsythe & J. Melling, *The Politics of Madness: The State, Insanity and Society in England, 1845–1914*, London, Routledge, 2006, p.1.
10. Wallace & Gach, *History of Psychiatry*, p.391.

Chapter 1

1. W. C. Oulton, *Picture of Margate and Its Vicinity*, London, Baldwin, Craddock & Joy, 1820, p.33.
2. Cited in A. Lee, 'The Sad Tale of the Margate Architect and the Brighton Poisoner,' p.1.
3. Lee, 'The Sad Tale of the Margate Architect and the Brighton Poisoner', p.2.
4. *Ibid*, pp.2–3.
5. L. Appignanesi, *Trials of Passion: Crimes in the Name of Love and Madness*, London, Virago, 2014, p.41.
6. W. Batcheller, *A Descriptive Picture of Dover; Or, the Visitors New Dover Guide*, Dover, W. Batcheller, 1838, p.14.
7. *Kentish Gazette*, 31 January 1831.
8. Batcheller, *New Dover Guide*, p.47, and Lee, 'The Sad Tale of the Margate Architect and the Brighton Poisoner', p.4.
9. Cited in Lee, 'The Sad Tale of the Margate Architect and the Brighton Poisoner', p.5.
10. P. Branca, *Silent Sisterhood: Middle Class Women in the Victorian Home*, Abingdon, Routledge, 2013, pp.40–45.
11. *The Times* 6 April 1842 & 2 May 1842.
12. *Morning Post*, 17 January 1842.
13. Lee, 'Sad Tale,' p.5.

14. Cited in L. Abrams, 'Ideals of Womanhood in Victorian Britain,' *BBC History*, http://www.bbc.co.uk/history/trail/victorian_britain/women_home/ideals_womanhood_01.shtml, 2001, n.p.
15. L. Davidoff & C. Hall, *Family Fortunes: Men and Women of the English Middle Class, 1780–1850*, Abingdon, Routledge, 2006, p.389.
16. See, for example, I. Beeton, *Beeton's Book of Household Management*, Ex-Classics Library, 2009, p.86, available at www.exclassics.com., &, C.Dickens Jr., *Dickens' Dictionary of London*, 1879, available at www.victorianlondon.org.
17. Davidoff & Hall, *Family Fortunes*, *p*.340.
18. O. Blouet, 'Public Schools,' in S. Mitchell (ed.), *Victorian Britain: An Encyclopedia*, Abingdon, Routledge, 2011, pp.651–2; Courtesy of King's School Archives.
19. Quoted in Branca, *Silent Sisterhood*.
20. F. Power Cobbe, *Life of Frances Power Cobbe: By Herself*, Cambridge, Riverside Press, 1894, pp.58–45, 56.
21. M. Somerville, *Personal Recollections From Early Life to Old Age of Mary Somerville With Selections From Her Correspondence*, London, John Murray, 1874, pp.21–24.
22. Cobbe, *Life of*, p.p.57–8.
23. *Ibid*, p.56.
24. *Ibid*, p.57.
25. *Ibid*, pp.59–60.
26. C. Dyhouse, *Girls Growing Up in Late Victorian and Edwardian England*, Abingdon, Routledge, 2013, p.54.
27. Cobbe, *Life of*, p.54.
28. *Ibid*, p.61.
29. D. Gorham, *The Victorian Girl and the Feminine Ideal*, Abingdon, Routledge, 2013, p.53.

Chapter 2
1. *Morning Post*, 17 January 1872.
2. W. A. F. Browne, *What Asylums Were, Are, and Ought To Be*, London, Longman, 1837, p. 169.
3. *Ibid*, p.101.
4. *Report of the Metropolitan Commissioners in Lunacy, to the Lord Chancellor*, London, Bradbury & Evans, 1844, see especially pp.54–55.
5. Cited in Lee, 'The Sad Tale of the Margate Architect and the Brighton Poisoner', pp. 7–8.
6. *Morning Post*, 17 January 1872.
7. *Ibid*.
8. Cited in W. L. Parry-Jones, *The Trade in Lunacy: A Study of Private Madhouses in England in the Eighteenth and Nineteenth Centuries*, Abingdon, Routledge, 1971, p.125.
9. *Morning Post*, 17 January 1872.
10. *The Times*, 4 July 1843.
11. *Report of the Metropolitan Commissioners*, p.44.
12. William Harnett Blanch, *Ye Parish of Camerwell; A Brief Account of the Parish of Camberwell, its History and Antiquities*, London, E. W. Allen, 1875, p.349.
13. *Further Report of the Metropolitan Commissioners in Lunacy, to the Lord Chancellor*, 1847, p. 347.
14. *Ibid*, p.352.
15. A. Digby, 'Tuke, William (1732–1822)', *Oxford Dictionary of National Biography*, Oxford University Press, 2004.

16. L. C. Charland, 'Benevolent Theory: Moral Treatment at the York Retreat', *History of Psychiatry*, vol. 18, no. 1, http://www.sagepub.com/pomerantzcpstudy/articles/Chapter02_Article01.pdf, 2007, pp.65–66.
17. J. Conolly, *The Treatment of the Insane Without Mechanical Restraint*, London, Smith, Elder & Co., 1856, pp. 50–51.
18. *Further Report of the Metropolitan Commissioners*, pp.435–436.
19. *Ibid*.
20. Conolly, *Treatment of the Insane*, p.72.
21. *Ibid*, p.69; *Further Report of the Metropolitan Commissioners*, pp. 343–5, 493.
22. *Further Report of the Metropolitan Commissioners*, p.435.
23. *Ibid*.
24. *Ibid*, p.493.
25. *Ibid*.
26. *Kentish Gazette*, 23 March 1847.
27. Prichard, *Treatise on Insanity*, pp.13–14,136–139
28. John C. Waller, 'Ideas of Heredity, Reproduction and Eugenics in Britain, 1800–1875,' *Studies in History and Philosophy of Biological and Biomedical Sciences*, vol. 32, No.3, p.460.
29. Prichard, *Treatise on Insanity*, p.123
30. Waller, 'Ideas of Heredity', p.460.
31. H. Bennett & T. Wakley (eds.), *The London Lancet*, New York, Burgess, Stringer & Co., 1845, p.493.
32. *The Literary Gazette; and Journal Of Belles Lettres, Arts, Sciences Etc.*, London, 1827, p.620.
33. Mitchell, *Daily Life*, p.155.
34. *Kentish Gazette*, 11 May 1847.
35. *Ibid*, 25 May 1847.

Chapter 3
1. M. Dobson, 'Population 1640–1831' and J. Preston, 'Industry 1800–1914,' in A. Armstrong (ed.), *The Economy of Kent, 1640–1914*, Boydell Press, Woodbridge, 1995, pp.15, 120.
2. The National Archives: PROB/11/2054/117.
3. *Ibid*.
4. M. J. Paterson, 'The Victorian Governess: Status Incongruence in Family and Society,' in M. Vicinus (ed.), *Suffer and Be Still: Women in the Victorian Age*, Abingdon, Routledge, 1972, pp.5–6.
5. Gorham, *The Victorian Girl*, pp.27–28.
6. Quoted in Paterson, 'The Victorian Governess', p.10.
7. *Ibid*, p.12.
8. A governess in this period could earn anywhere between £15 and £100 per year but these figures represent the average, and most realistic, earnings.
9. *Ibid*, pp.7–8.
10. Mitchell, *Victorian Britain*, p.336.
11. H. Maudsley & J. Sibbald, *The Journal of Mental Science: Volume 18*, London, J. A. Churchill & Son, 1873, pp.104–105.
12. Quoted in A. Mangham, 'Hysterical Fictions,' *The Wilkie Collins Journal*, http://wilkiecollinssociety.org/hysterical-fictions-mid-nineteenth-century-medical-constructions-of-hysteria-and-the-fiction-of-mary-elizabeth-braddon/, 2003, n.p.

13. 'Hysteria', *Science Museum*, http://www.sciencemuseum.org.uk/broughttolife/themes/menalhealthandillness/~/link.aspx?_id=D300E3E638A847DBBDA462366A03D41A&_z=z, n.p.
14. F. C. Skey, *Hysteria: Six Lectures*, New York; Moorhead, Simpson & Bond; 1866, p.41.
15. Mangham, 'Hysterical Fictions,' n.p.
16. G. Tate, *A Treatise on Hysteria*, London, 1830, pp.11–12.
17. Prichard, *Treatise on Insanity*, p.157.
18. *Ibid.*
19. Mangham, 'Hysterical Fictions,' n.p.
20. J. Althaus, *On Epilepsy, Hysteria, and Ataxy: Three Lectures*, London John Churchill & Sons, 1866, p.39.
21. Maudsley & Sibbald, *The Journal of Mental Science*, p.104.
22. Althaus, *On Epilepsy*, pp.53–55.
23. *Ibid*, pp.65–67.
24. *Ibid.*
25. A. Tweedie, *A System of Practical Medicine Comprised in a Series of Original Dissertations*, London, Whittaker & Co., 1840, pp.228–229.
26. Quoted in I. Morus, *Shocking Bodies: Life, Death and Electricity in Victorian England*, Stroud, The History Press, 2011, pp.89–91.
27. R. P. Maines, *The Technology of Orgasm: "Hysteria", the Vibrator and Women's Sexual Satisfaction*, Baltimore, John Hopkins University Press, 1999, pp.1, 24.
28. *Morning Post*, 17 January 1872.
29. Maudsley & Sibbald, *Journal of Mental Science*, p.105.
30. Quoted in O. Temkin, *The Falling Sickness: A History of Epilepsy From the Greeks to the Beginnings of Modern Neurology*, www.books.google.co.uk, 2010, n.p.
31. G Davis, *"The Cruel Madness of Love": Sex, Syphilis and Psychiatry in Scotland, 1880–1930*, Amsterdam, Rodopi, 2008, pp.199–200.
32. Wallace & Gach, *History of Psychiatry*, p.391.
33. M. Wilson Carpenter, *Health, Medicine and Society in Victorian England*, California, ABC-CLIO, 2010, p.90.
34. *Ibid*, p. 89.
35. C. Hutto & G. B. Scott, *Congenital and Perinatal Infections: A Concise Guide to Diagnosis*, New Jersey, Humana, www.books.google.co.uk, 2006, p.200.
36. *Who Do You Think You Are*, Series 6, Episode 11, BBC Television, London, Broadcast 2010.
37. J. MacIntyre & M. L. Newell, *Congenital and Perinatal Infections: Prevention, Diagnosis and Treatment*, Cambridge, Cambridge University Press, 2000, p.268.
38. J. Marazzo & C. Celum, 'Syphilis in Women', in M. Goldman, R. Troisi & K. Rexrode, *Women and Health: Second Edition*, London, Elsevier, 2013, p.469.
39. M. R. Khan & M. Ekhlasur Rahman, *Essence of Pediatrics*, London, Elsevier, www.books.google.co.uk, 2011, p.398.
40. Hutto & Scott, *Congenital and Perinatal Infections*, p.201.
41. 'Hydrocephalus', *National Institute of Neurological Disorders and Stroke*, http://www.ninds.nih.gov/disorders/hydrocephalus/detail_hydrocephalus.htm, 2015, n.p.

Chapter 4

1. *The Times*, March 26 1867.
2. C. M. Oslund, *Disability Services and Disability Studies in Higher Education: History Contexts and Social Impacts*, Basingstoke, Palgrave MacMillan, 2015, pp.43–44.
3. *The Times*, 22 June 1860.

4. Maudsley & Sibbald, *The Journal of Mental Science,* pp.104, 106.
5. 'The Earlswood Asylum for Idiots', *Langdon-Down Museum of Learning* Disability, http://langdondownmuseum.org.uk/dr-john-langdon-down-and-normansfield/the-earlswood-asylum-for-idiots/, n.p.
6. Maudsley & Sibbald, *Journal of Mental Science,* p.104
7. D. Barltrop & B. K. Sandhu, 'Marasmus,' *Postgraduate Medical Journal,* Volume 61, http://pmj.bmj.com/content/61/720/915.full.pdf+html, 1985, pp.919–920.
8. D. Marshall, *Industrial England, 1776–1851,* Abingdon, Routledge, 2006, pp.54–55.
9. *Ibid,* p. 55;, 'The History of Brighton's Tourism,' *Visit Brighton,* https://www.visitbrighton.com/xsdbimgs/history%20of%20brighton%20tourism.pdf, p.2.
10. *Morning Post,* 25 August 1871.
11. N. P. Blaker, *Sussex in Bygone Days: The Reminiscences of Nathaniel Paine Blaker, M. R. C. S.,* http://freepages.genealogy.rootsweb.ancestry.com/~blaker/reminiscences/contents.html, p.51.
12. E. Burke, *The Annual Register,* London, Rivingtons, 1873, p.197.
13. Maudsley & Sibbald, *Journal of Mental Science,* p.105.
14. *Ibid,* p.105.
15. J. Delaney, M. J. Lupton & E. Toth, *The Curse: A Cultural History of Menstruation,* Illinois, University of Illinois Press, 1988, p.220.
16. E. J. Tilt, *The Change of Life in Health and Disease: A Practical Treatise on the Nervous and Other Affections Incidental to Women at the Decline of Life,* Philadelphia, Lindsay & Blackiston, 1871, pp.26–27.
17. *The Times,* 14 September 1871.
18. A. Broomfield, *Food and Cooking in Victorian England: A History,* Westport, Greenwood Publishing Group, 2007, p. 117.; S. Morton, 'A Little of What You Fancy Does You… Harm!', in J. Rowbotham & K. Stevenson (eds.), *Criminal Conversations Victorian Crimes, Social Panic and Moral Outrage,* Ohio, Ohio State University, 2005, pp.161–162.
19. J, Emsley, *The Elements of Murder: A History of Poison,* Oxford, Oxford University Press, 2005, pp.100–101.
20. E. Burke, *The Annual Register,* London, Rivingtons, 1860, pp.198–199.
21. Broomfield, *Food and Cooking,* p.117.; Morton, 'A Little of What You Fancy', pp.161–162.
22. *The Star,* 14 September 1871.

Chapter 5
1. *Daily News,* 9 September 1871.
2. K. Watkins, *Poisoned Lives: English Poisoners and Their Victims,* Hambledon, London, 2004, p.33.
3. *Ibid,* p.34.
4. *The Times,* 22 July 1869, 6 August 1869.
5. R. N. Karmakar, *Forensic Medicine and Toxicology,* India, Academic Publishers, www.books.google.co.uk, 2010, pp.84, 122; J. C. Whorton, *The Arsenic Century: How Victorian Britain was Poisoned at Home, Work & Play,* Oxford, Oxford University Press, 2010, p.10.
6. J. Buckingham, *Bitter Nemesis: The Intimate History of Strychnine,* London, CRC Press, 2008, pp.67–69.
7. Watkins, *Poisoned Lives,* p.33.
8. *The Times,* 11 February 1859.
9. *Manchester Times,* 26 February 1871.
10. E. Cresy, *On a Preliminary Enquiry into the Sewerage, Drainage and Supply of Water, and the Sanitary Condition of the Inhabitants of the Town of Brighton,* London, William Clowes and Son, 1849, p.10.

11. J. M. Eyler, *Sir Arthur Newsholme and State Medicine: 1885–1935*, Cambridge, Cambridge University Press, 1997, pp.9–12.
12. Quoted in R. Collis, *Death and the City: the Nation's Experience, Told Through Brighton's History*, Brighton, Hanover Press, 2013, p.93.
13. *Daily News*, 16 January 1872.
14. *Daily News*, 25 August 1871; Buckingham, *Bitter Nemesis*, p.70. According to Buckingham, there are recorded instances of an adult dying after ingesting as little as one-half of a grain of strychnine.
15. *The Times*, 1 September 1871.

Chapter 6
1. *Daily News*, 16 January 1872.
2. *The Times*, 8 September 1871.
3. *Ibid.*
4. *Daily News*, 16 January 1872; 'Poisoning By Strychnia in Sweetmeats,' *The Pharmaceutical Journal*, London, J & A. Churchill, https://archive.org/stream/pharmaceuticaljo2187phar/pharmaceuticaljo2187phar_djvu.txt, 1872, p.16.
5. *The Times*, 8 September 1871.
6. Watkins, *Poisoned Lives*, p.167.
7. *Brighton Gazette*, 29 June 1871.
8. *Ibid*, p.27.
9. *Daily News*, 25 August 1871.
10. 'Poisoning By Strychnia,'pp.16–18.

Chapter 7
1. The author has been unable to locate this letter.
2. *Morning Post*, 16 January 1872.
3. *Nottinghamshire Guardian*, 1 September 1871.
4. *Morning Post*, 17 January 1872; Maudsley & Sibbald, *Journal of Mental Science*, p.105.
5. T. Page, *Folthorp's General Directory for Brighton, Hove and Cliftonville*, Brighton, Thomas Page, 1864.
6. *Nottinghamshire Guardian*, 1 September 1871.

Chapter 8
1. *Daily News*, 25 August 1871.
2. *Morning Post*, 17 January 1872.
3. Blaker, *Sussex in Bygone Days*, p.51.
4. *Manchester Times*, 2 September 1871.
5. Blaker, *Sussex in Bygone Days*, p.51.
6. *Ibid.*
7. *Manchester Times*, 2 September 1871.
8. This is based on a lethal dose of four to five grains of arsenic, equivalent to 259.2 mg, as quoted in Whorton, *Arsenic Century*, p.10.
9. Maudsley & Sibbald, *Journal of Mental Science*, p.105.
10. *Daily News*, 25 August 1871.
11. *The Times*, 18 August 1871.
12. *Manchester Times*, 26 August 1871.

Chapter 9
1. *Daily News*, 25 August 1871.
2. *Manchester Times* 26 August 1871.

3. *Evening Gazette*, 25 August 1871.
4. *Manchester Times*, 26 August 1871.
5. *Ibid.*
6. Quoted in Whorton, *Arsenic Century*, p.1.
7. Watkins, *Poisoned Lives*, p.47.
8. *Manchester Times*, 26 Aug 1871.
9. *Daily News*, 25 August 1871.
10. *Ibid.*
11. 'Experts in Handwriting', *The Cornhill Magazine*, Vol. 4, London, Smith, Elder & Co., 1885, p.151.
12. *Morning Post*, 1 September 1871.
13. See *Morning Post*, 21 July 1863 for Netherclift's testimony.
14. *Morning Post*, 1 September 1871.
15. *Morning Post*, 21 July 1863.
16. *Morning Post*, 1 September 1871.
17. *Reynold's Newspaper*, 10 July 1870.
18. *Belfast Newsletter*, 22 November 1869.
19. *Morning Post*, 1 September 1871.
20. *The Star*, 5 September 1871.
21. *Morning Post*, 8 & 9 September 1871.
22. *The Star*, 14 September 1871.
23. *Ibid.*
24. *The Star*, 14 September 1871.
25. 'The Brighton Poisoning Case,' *The Chemist and Druggist*, 15 September 1871, p.298.
26. *Evening Gazette*, 2 January 1872.
27. *Lancaster Gazette*, 25 November 1871.
28. *Evening Gazette*, 2 January 1872.
29. *Hastings and St Leonard's Observer*, 12 August 1871.
30. *Ibid.*
31. *Ibid.*
32. *Ibid.*
33. *Lancaster Gazette*, 25 November 1871.

Chapter 10
1. D. Defoe, *The Fortunes and Misfortunes of the Famous Moll Flanders*, Minneapolis, Lerner, 2014, p.281.
2. H. Mayhew & J. Binny, *The Criminal Prisons of London and Scenes of Prison Life*, London; Griffin, Bohn & Company, 1862, pp.593–594.
3. *The Times*, 30 December 1871.
4. 'Eva Pierlo', T. Hitchcock, R. Shoemaker, C. Emsley, S. Howard, & J. McLaughlin, *et al.*, *The Old Bailey Proceedings Online, 1674–1913, http://www.oldbaileyonline.org/browse.jsp?path=sessionsPapers%2F18720108.xml*; *Morning Post*, 10 January 1872; *The Times*, 10 January 1872.
5. *Pall Mall Gazette*, 1 January 1872.
6. Mayhew & Binny, *Criminal Prisons of London*, pp.597–598, 604.
7. J. A. Hamilton, 'Parry, John Humffreys (1816–1880), *Oxford Dictionary of National Biography*, Oxford, Oxford University Press, 2004.
8. C. Elliott, *The Rules of Insanity: Moral Responsibility and the Mentally Ill Offender*, New York, State University of New York, 1996, pp.10–11.

9. *Morning Post*, 17 January 1872.
10. *The Times*, 18 January 1872.
11. Prichard, *Treatise on Insanity*, pp.16, 28–29.
12. *The Era*, 14 January 1872.
13. *Illustrated Police News*, 20 January 1872.
14. *Daily News*, 16 January 1872.
15. *Ibid.*
16. *Ibid.*
17. *Morning Post*, 17 January 1872.
18. *Ibid.*
19. *Ibid.*

Chapter 11
1. *Illustrated Police News*, 20 January 1872.
2. Blaker, *Sussex in Bygone Days*, n.p.
3. *The Times*, 20 January 1872.
4. *Morning Post, 5 February 1872.*
5. *Ibid.*
6. *Reynold's Newspaper*, 28 January 1872.
7. *Huddersfield Chronicle and West Yorkshire Advertiser*, 27 January 1872.
8. *The Era*, 21 January 1872.
9. *Illustrated Police News*, 20 January 1872.
10. See *Pall Mall Gazette*, 25 January 1872.
11. M. J. Wiener, *Men of Blood: Violence, Manliness and Criminal Justice in Victorian England*, Cambridge, Cambridge University Press, 2006, p.13
12. Information based on research carried out by Richard Clark, Dave Mossop & Matthew Spicer for the website Capital Punishment UK (www.capitalpunishmentuk.org).
13. Wiener, *Men of Blood*, p.133.
14. *Manchester Times*, 27 January 1872.
15. *Pall Mall Gazette*, 19 January 1872.
16. *The Times*, 17 January 1872.
17. Quoted in A. Mangham, *Violent Women and Sensation Fiction: Crime, Medicine and Victorian Popular Culture*, London, Palgrave, 2007, pp.36–37.
18. *Derby Mercury*, 31 January 1872.
19. *Reynold's Newspaper*, 28 January 1872.
20. *Morning Post*, 31 January 1872.
21. *Derby Mercury*, 31 January 1872.
22. *Bedford Times and Bedfordshire Independent*, 27 January 1872.
23. L. Appignanesi, *Trials of Passion: Crimes in the Name of Love and Madness*, London, Virago, 2014, pp.116–117.
24. *York Herald*, 25 May 1872.
25. *South Eastern Advertiser*, 19 October 1872 & *Whitstable Times and Herne Bay Herald*, 27 November 1875.
26. Berkshire Record Office: D/H/14/D2/2/2/204/1
27. Berkshire Record Office: D/H14/D2/1/2/1

Chapter 12
1. *The Times*, 13 January 1865.
2. *Reports From Committees: Sixteen Volumes*, Volume XXII, 1860, p.xiv.

3. M. Stevens, *Broadmoor Revealed: Victorian Crime and the Lunatic Asylum*, Barnsley, Pen & Sword, 2013, p.7.
4. *Ibid*, p. 8.
5. See, for example, Lucia Zedner, *Women, Crime and Custody in Victorian England*, Oxford, Oxford University Press, 1991.
6. A. Cossins, *Female Criminality: Infanticide, Moral Panic and the Female Body*, Basingstoke, Palgrave Macmillan, 2015, pp.193,197.
7. Stevens, *Inside Broadmoor*, pp.119–122.
8. H. Deacon, 'The Medical Institutions on Robben Island, 1846–1931,' in H. Deacon (ed.), *The Island: A History of Robben Island, 1488–1990*, Claremont, David Philip, 1996, pp.66–67; 'Dr William Edmunds,' *Biographical Database of South African Science*, http://www.s2a3.org.za/bio/Biograph_final.php?serial=841, 2014.
9. Berkshire Record Office: D/H14/D2/1/2/1.
10. Berkshire Record Office: D/H14/D2/2/2/204/ p.3 & 5.
11. Berkshire Record Office: D/H14/D2/1/2/1.
12. Stevens, *Broadmoor Revealed*, pp.7,15–19.
13. Berkshire Record Office: D/H14/D2/1/2/1.
14. Quoted in Appignanesi, *Trials of Passion*, p.132.
15. Stevens, *Broadmoor Revealed*, pp.24–25.
16. Berkshire Record Office: D/H14/D2/1/2/1.
17. *Yorkshire Telegraph and Star*, 28 September 1907.
18. See, for example, *Cheltenham Chronicle*, 28 September 1907 and *Manchester Courier*, 28 September 1907.

Epilogue
1. *Inside Broadmoor*, Series 1, Episode 1, television programme, Channel 5, London, Broadcast 30 September 2013.
2. C. Malmquist, *Homicide: A Psychiatric Perspective*, Arlington, American Psychiatric Press, 2006, pp.177–179.
3. *Ibid*, p.179.
4. 'Personality Disorders,' *Mental Health Foundation*, http://www.mentalhealth.org.uk/help-information/mental-health-a-z/P/personality-disorders/, 2015.
5. A. Tomkins, 'Mad Doctors? The Significance of Medical Practitioners Admitted as Patients to the First English County Asylums up to 1890,' in *History of Psychiatry*, vol. 23(4), pp.437–453; A. Tomkins, 'Case Notes and Madness,' in M. Jackson (ed.), *Routledge History of Disease*, London, Routledge, Forthcoming.
6. Berkshire Record Office: D/H14/D2/1/2/1.

Bibliography

Primary Sources

Archives
For Willam Edmunds' will, please see: The National Archives: PROB/11/2054/117.
For William Edmunds' school record, please see the Archives of the King's School, Canterbury.
For Christiana's case file from Broadmoor, please see: Berkshire Record Office: D/H/14/
    D2/2/2/204 and D/H14/D2/1/2/1.

Newspapers
All newspapers consulted in this book are available to view on the British Newspaper Archives
(www.britishnewspaperarchive.co.uk), The Times Digital Archive and 19th Century British
Newspapers (www.gale.cengage.co.uk). The only exception is the *Brighton Gazette* which is
available to view on microfiche in The Keep, Brighton.

Books
Please note the following books are freely available to view at Google Books (www.books.
google.com) and Internet Archive (www.archive.org).

Althaus, J., *On Epilepsy, Hysteria, and Ataxy: Three Lectures*, London John Churchill & Sons,
    1866.
Batcheller, William., *A Descriptive Picture of Dover; Or, the Visitors New Dover Guide*, Dover,
    W. Batcheller, 1838.
Bennet, H. & T. Wakley (eds.), *The London Lancet*, New York, Burgess, Stringer & Co., 1845.
Bonner, G. W., *The Picturesque Pocket Companion to Margate, Broadstairs, and Parts Adjacent*,
    London, William Kidd, 1831.
'The Brighton Poisoning Case,' *The Chemist and Druggist*, 15 September 1871.
Browne, W. A. F., *What Asylums Were, Are, and Ought To Be*, London, Longman, 1837.
Burke. E., *The Annual Register*, London, Rivingtons, 1873
Cobbe, F. P., *Life of Frances Power Cobbe: By Herself*, Cambridge, Riverside Press, 1894.
Conolly, J., *The Treatment of the Insane Without Mechanical Restraint*, London, Smith, Elder
    & Co., 1856.
Cresy, E., *On a Preliminary Enquiry into the Sewerage, Drainage and Supply of Water, and the
    Sanitary Condition of the Inhabitants of the Town of Brighton*, London, William Clowes and
    Son, 1849.
—— 'Experts in Handwriting,' *The Cornhill Magazine*, Vol. 4, London, Smith, Elder & Co.,
    1885, pp.148–162.
—— *Further Report of the Metropolitan Commissioners in Lunacy, to the Lord Chancellor*,
    London, Bradbury & Evans, 1847.

Hamilton, J. A., 'Parry, John Humffreys (1816–1880), *Oxford Dictionary of National Biography*, Oxford, Oxford University Press, 2004.

Harnett Blanch, W., *Ye Parish of Camerwell; A Brief Account of the Parish of Camberwell, its History and Antiquities*, London, E. W. Allen, 1875.

Hitchcock, T, R. Shoemaker, C. Emsley, S. Howard, & J. McLaughlin, et al., *The Old Bailey Proceedings Online, 1674–1913, http://www.oldbaileyonline.org*, (accessed March 2015).

Maudsley, H. & J. Sibbald, *The Journal of Mental Science: Volume 18*, London, J. A. Churchill & Son, 1873.

Mayhew, H. & J. Binny, *The Criminal Prisons of London and Scenes of Prison Life*, London; Griffin, Bohn & Company, 1862.

Oulton, Walley Chamberlain, *Picture of Margate and Its Vicinity*, London, Baldwin, Cradock & Joy, 1820.

Page, T., *Folthorp's General Directory for Brighton, Hove and Cliftonville*, Brighton, Thomas Page, 1864.

'Poisoning By Sweetmeats,' *Pharmaceutical Journal*, London, J. & A. Churchill, 1872, pp.16–18.

Prichard, J. C., *A Treatise on Insanity and Other Disorders Affecting the Mind*, Philadelphia, Carey & Hart, 1837.

—— *Report of the Metropolitan Commissioners in Lunacy, to the Lord Chancellor*, London, Bradbury & Evans, 1844.

—— *Reports From Committees: Sixteen Volumes*, Volume XXII, 1860.

Skey, F. C., *Hysteria: Six Lectures*, New York; Moorhead, Simpson & Bond, 1866.

Somerville, M., *Personal Recollections From Early Life to Old Age of Mary Somerville With Selections From Her Correspondence*, London, John Murray, 1874.

Tate, G., *A Treatise on Hysteria*, London, 1830.

—— *The Literary Gazette; and Journal Of Belles Lettres, Arts, Sciences Etc.*, London, 1827.

Tilt, E, J,, *The Change of Life in Health and Disease: A Practical Treatise on the Nervous and Other Affections Incidental to Women at the Decline of Life*, Philadelphia, Lindsay & Blackiston, 1871.

Tweedie, A., *A System of Practical Medicine Comprised in a Series of Original Dissertations*, London, Whittaker & Co., 1840.

Secondary Sources

Abrams, L. 'Ideals of Womanhood in Victorian Britain,' *BBC History*, http://www.bbc. co.uk/history/trail/victorian_britain/women_home/ideals_womanhood_01.shtml, 2001, (accessed June 2014).

Appignanesi, L., *Trials of Passion: Crimes in the Name of Love and Madness*, London, Virago, 2014.

Barltrop D.& B. K. Sandhu, 'Marasmus,' *Postgraduate Medical Journal*, Volume 61, available at http://pmj.bmj.com/content/61/720/915.full.pdf+html, 1985, pp.915–923.

Blaker, N. P., *Sussex in Bygone Days: The Reminiscences of Nathaniel Paine Blaker, M. R. C. S.*, Hove, Combridges, http://freepages.genealogy.rootsweb.ancestry.com/~blaker/reminiscences/contents.html, (accessed November 2014).

Blouet, O., 'Public Schools,' in Mitchell, S. (ed.), *Victorian Britain: An Encyclopedia*, Abingdon, Routledge, 2011, pp.650–652.

Branca, P., *Silent Sisterhood: Middle Class Women in the Victorian Home*, Abingdon, Routledge, 2013.

Brewitt Brown, J., 'Class and Money', in Bloom, H. (ed.), *The Victorian Novel*, (New York, Chelsea House, 2004) pp.69–90.

Broomfield, A., *Food and Cooking in Victorian England: A History*, Westport, Greenwood Publishing, 2007.

Buckingham, J., *Bitter Nemesis: The Intimate History of Strychnine*, London, CRC Press, 2008.

Charland, L. C., 'Benevolent Theory: Moral Treatment at the York Retreat', *History of Psychiatry*, vol. 18, no. 1, http://www.sagepub.com/pomerantzcpstudy/articles/Chapter02_Article01.pdf, 2007, (accessed June 2014).

Collis, R., *Death and the City: the Nation's Experience, Told Through Brighton's History*, Brighton, Hanover Press, 2013.

Cossins, A., *Female Criminality: Infanticide, Moral Panic and the Female Body*, Basingstoke, Palgrave Macmillan, 2015.

Davis, G., *"The Cruel Madness of Love": Sex, Syphilis and Psychiatry in Scotland, 1880–1930*, Amsterdam, Rodopi, 2008.

Davis G., 'The Most Deadly Disease of Asylumdom: General Paralysis of the Insane and Scottish Psychiatry, c.1840–1890,' *Journal of the Royal College of Physicians Edinburgh*, vol.42, no.3, 2012, http://www.rcpe.ac.uk/sites/default/files/davis.pdf (accessed June 2014).

Davidoff, L. & C. Hall, *Family Fortunes: Men and Women of the English Middle Class, 1780–1850*, Abingdon, Routledge, 2006.

Deacon, H., 'The Medical Institutions on Robben Island, 1846–1931,' in Deacon, H. (ed.), *The Island: A History of Robben Island, 1488–1990*, Claremont, David Philip, 1996, pp.57–75.

Defoe, D., *The Fortunes and Misfortunes of the Famous Moll Flanders*, Minneapolis, Lerner, 2014.

Delaney, J., M. J. Lupton & E. Toth, *The Curse: A Cultural History of Menstruation*, Illinois, University of Illinois Press, 1988.

Digby, A., 'Tuke, William (1732–1822)', *Oxford Dictionary of National Biography*, Oxford University Press, www.oxforddnb.com, 2004, (accessed June 2014).

Dobson, M., 'Population 1640–1831' and Preston, A., 'Industry 1800–1914,' in A. Armstrong (ed.), *The Economy of Kent, 1640–1914*, Boydell Press, Woodbridge, 1995, pp.5–29,110–124.

'Dr William Edmunds,' *Biographical Database of South African Science*, http://www.s2a3.org.za/bio/Biograph_final.php?serial=841, 2014, (accessed December 2014).

Dyhouse, C., *Girls Growing Up in Late Victorian and Edwardian England*, Abingdon, Routledge, 2013.

'The Earlswood Asylum for Idiots,' *Langdon-Down Museum of Learning Disability*, available at http://langdondownmuseum.org.uk/dr-john-langdon-down-and-normansield/the-earlswood-asylum-for-idiots/, (accessed January 2015).

Emsley, J., *The Elements of Murder: A History of Poison*, Oxford, Oxford University Press, 2005.

Eyler, J. M., *Sir Arthur Newsholme and State Medicine: 1885–1935*, Cambridge, Cambridge University Press, 1997.

Forsythe, B & Melling, J., *The Politics of Madness: The State, Insanity and Society in England, 1845–1914*, London, Routledge, 2006.

Frost, G., *Victorian Childhoods*, Westport, Greenwood, 2009.

Gorham, D., *The Victorian Girl and the Feminine Ideal*, Abingdon, Routledge, 2013.

Haslam, F. *From Hogarth to Rowlandson: Medicine in Art in Eighteenth-Century Britain*, Liverpool, Liverpool University Press, 1996.

'The History of Brighton's Tourism,' *Visit Brighton*, available at https://www.visitbrighton.com/xsdbimgs/history%20of%20brighton%20tourism.pdf, (accessed December 2014).

Hutto, C., & G. B. Scott, *Congenital and Perinatal Infections: A Concise Guide to Diagnosis,* New Jersey, Humana, avaialbe at www.books.google.co.uk, 2010, (accessed January 2015).

'Hydrocephalus', *National Institute of Neurological Disorders and Stroke, http://www.ninds.nih.gov/disorders/hydrocephalus/detail_hydrocephalus.htm,* 2015, (date accessed January 2015).

'Hysteria,' *Science Museum,* http://www.sciencemuseum.org.uk/broughttolife/themes/menalhealthandillness/~/link.aspx?_id=D300E3E638A847DBBDA462366A03D41A&_z=z, (date accessed July 2014).

Karmakar, R. N., *Forensic Medicine and Toxicology,* India, Academic Publishers, available at www.books.google.co.uk, 2010, (accessed December 2014).

Inside Broadmoor, Series 1, Episode 1, television programme, Channel 5, London, Broadcast 30 September 2013.

Khan, M. R. & M. Ekhlasur Rahman, *Essence of Pediatrics,* London, Elsevier, available at www.books.google.co.uk, 2011, (accessed January 2011).

Lee, A., 'The Sad Tale of the Margate Architect and the Brighton Poisoner,' http://www.margatelocalhistory.co.uk/Articles/Edmunds%20tale.pdf, (accessed June 2014).

MacIntyre, J., & M. L. Newell, *Congenital and Perinatal Infections: Prevention, Diagnosis and Treatment,* Cambridge, Cambridge University Press, 2000.

Maines, R. P., *The Technology of Orgasm: "Hysteria," the Vibrator and Women's Sexual Satisfaction,* Baltimore, John Hopkins Press, 1999.

Malmquist, C., *Homicide: A Psychiatric Perspective,* Arlington, American Psychiatric Press, 2006.

Mangham, A., 'Hysterical Fictions,' *The Wilkie Collins Journal, http://wilkiecollinssociety.org/hysterical-fictions-mid-nineteenth-century-medical-constructions-of-hysteria-and-the-fiction-of-mary-elizabeth-braddon/,* 2003, (accessed July 2014).

Mangham, A., *Violent Women and Sensation Fiction: Crime, Medicine and Victorian Popular Culture,* London, Palgrave, 2007.

Marazzo, J., & C. Celum, 'Syphilis in Women', in M. Goldman, R. Troisi & K. Rexrode, *Women and Health: Second Edition,* London, Elsevier, 2013.

Marshall, D., *Industrial England, 1776–1851,* Abingdon, Routledge, 2006.

Mitchell, S., *Daily Life in Victorian England,* Westport, Greenwood, 1996.

Morus, I., *Shocking Bodies: Life, Death & Electricity in Victorian England,* Stroud, The History Press, 2011.

Morton, S., 'A Little of What You Fancy Does You...Harm!', in J. Rowbotham & K. Stevenson (eds.), *Criminal Conversations: Victorian Crimes, Social Panic and Moral Outrage,* Ohio, Ohio State University, 2005,pp.157–176.

Nelson, C., *Family Ties in Victorian England,* Wesport, Greenwood, 2007.

Oslund, C. M., *Disability Services and Disability Studies in Higher Education: History Contexts and Social Impacts,* Basingstoke, Palgrave MacMillan, 2015.

Parry-Jones, W. L., *The Trade in Lunacy: A Study of Private Madhouses in England in the Eighteenth and Nineteenth Centuries,* Abingdon, Routledge, 1971.

Paterson, M. J., 'The Victorian Governess: Status Incongruence in Family and Society,' in Vicinus, M., (ed.), *Suffer and Be Still: Women in the Victorian Age,* Abingdon, Routledge, 1972, pp.3–19.

—— 'Personality Disorders,' *Mental Health Foundation,* http://www.mentalhealth.org.uk/help-information/mental-health-a-z/P/personality-disorders/, 2015, (accessed June 2014).

Stevens, M., *Broadmoor Revealed: Victorian Crime and the Lunatic Asylum,* Barnsley, Pen & Sword, 2013.

Stevens, M., *Life in the Victorian Asylum: The World of Nineteenth-Century Mental Health Care*, Barnsley, Pen & Sword, 2014.

Temkin, O., *The Falling Sickness: A History of Epilepsy From the Greeks to the Beginnings of Modern Neurology*, available at www.books.google.co.uk, 2010.

Thompson, F. M. L., *The Rise of Respectable Society: A Social History of Victorian Britain 1830–1900*, Harvard, Harvard University Press, 1990.

Tomkins, A., 'Mad Doctors? The Significance of Medical Practitioners Admitted as Patients to the First English County Asylums up to 1890,' in *History of Psychiatry*, Vol. 23(4), pp.437–453.

Tomkins, A., 'Case Notes and Madness,' in M. Jackson (ed.), *Routledge History of Disease*, London, Routledge, Forthcoming.

Wallace, E. R. IV & J. Gach (eds.), *History of Psychiatry and Medical Psychology*, New York, Springer Science and Business Media, 2008.

Waller, J. C., 'Ideas of Heredity, Reproduction and Eugenics in Britain, 1800–1875,' *Studies in History and Philosophy of Biological and Biomedical Sciences*, vol.32, No.3, www.ingentaconnect.com, 2001, (accessed June 2014).

Wallis, J., 'This Fascinating and Fatal Disease,' *The Psychologist*, vol 5, no. 10, http://www.thepsychologist.org.uk/ 2010, (accessed June 2014).

Watkins, K., *Poisoned Lives: English Poisoners and Their Victims*, Hambledon, London, 2004.

Who Do You Think You Are, Series 6, Episode 11, BBC Television, London, Broadcast 2010.

Whorton, J. C., *The Arsenic Century: How Victorian Britain was Poisoned at Home, Work & Play*, Oxford, Oxford University Press, 2010.

Wiener, M. J., *Men of Blood: Violence, Manliness and Criminal Justice in Victorian England*, Cambridge, Cambridge University Press, 2006.

Wilson Carpenter, M., *Health, Medicine and Society in Victorian England*, California, ABC-CLIO, 2010.

Index

Act to Regulate the Care and Treatment of Insane Persons in England, 15
Adulteration of Food and Drink Act, 47
Agate, Emily, 86–87, 94
Albert Terrace, 83
Althaus, Dr. Julian, 30
Armstrong, Dr Peter, 16
Arsenic, 46–47, 50, 61, 62, 79, 80, 93, 94–95, 100
  popularity of, 50
  Marsh Test, 50–1
  Reinsch Test, 51
  fatal dose, 51
  purchase of, 52
  symptoms of arsenic poisoning, 86–87
  see also, Christiana Edmunds, Poisoning

Baker, Emily, 55–56, 101
  family of, 55–56
Ballantine, William, 114–115, 118–119
Barker, Albert, 72–76, 101
Barker, Selicia, 59, 60
Barker, Sidney, 59–60, 61, 62–65, 67–68, 101, 114
  death, 60, 68, 74, 78, 81
Barming Heath Lunatic Asylum, 12
Beard, Dr. Charles, 41, 43, 44, 64, 66, 71, 86, 120, 121–122, 129, 136, 138, 144
  education, 41
  career, 41
  marriage, 44
  children, 44
  relationship with Christiana, 42–43, 45–46, 47–48, 76, 90, 101–102
  refuses to attend Christiana, 88–89
  interview with Inspector Gibbs, 90
  in court, 101–102
  flees to Scotland, 103
  at trial, 114–115
  in asylum, 144–145
  death 145
  see also, Christiana Edmunds, Emily Beard

Beard, Emily, 50, 64, 70, 71, 90–91
  marriage, 44
  children, 44
  relationship with Christiana, 44–45, 68–69
  poisoning of, 44–45, 48, 50, 51, 52, 84–85, 95, 102
  flees to Scotland, 103
  in court, 93–94, 101
  later years, 145
  death, 145
  see also, Dr. Charles Beard, Christiana Edmunds
Bearlings, Mrs, 83–84
Bethlem Hospital, vii, 22, 132
Black, David, 61, 62, 64, 65, 67–68, 78–80, 94, 114, 130
  see also, Coroner
Blaker, Nathaniel Paine, 86–87, 94, 95, 121
Boys, Elizabeth, 85, 86–87, 90, 97, 124
Boys, Jacob, 85
Bradbury, Samuel, 80
Bradshaw, Julian Watson, 38
  engagement, 38
  marriage, 39
  moves to Margate, 39
Bradshaw (née Edmunds), Louisa, (Christiana's sister), 36, 82, 83
  birth, 3
  career as a governess, 26, 28, 33, 38–39
  hysteria, 33, 39
  engagement, 38
  marriage, 39
  moves to Margate, 39
  death, 39, 116, 126
Bragnor, Robert, 58
Brayn, Dr. Richard, 140, 141
Brighton, 40, 55, 58, 59, 63, 76, 77, 80, 81, 92, 94, 122, 128, 130, 142
  development of, 40, 50
    under King George IV, 40
    under Queen Victoria, 40
  popularity of, 41, 144

Brighton Police Court, 92
Brighton Police Force, 60–61, 89
Brighton Rail Station, 82
Broadmoor Criminal Lunatic Asylum, 128,
    129, 131, 143
    description, 132
    history, 132
    types of patient, 134
    treatments, 135–136
    difficulties with Christiana, 136, 137
    daily routine, 137–138
    see also, Christiana Edmunds
Brooks, George, 101
Browne, Dr William A. F., 13
    condition of early private madhouses, 13
Bruce, Henry Austin, 125, 126, 127, 128,
    129, 139
Burn, Ellen, 43–44
Burn, Major John, 3, 43
Burn, John Southerden, 43
Burns, Robert, 69
Burrows, James Cordy, 128,
    complaints against Christiana, 128–129, 130

Canterbury, 24, 25, 28, 30, 130
Casanova, 106
Central Criminal Court (Old Bailey), 105,
    112, 129
    description of, 112–113
Central Criminal Court Act, 105
    see also, William Palmer
Charriere, Angelina, 7
Child, Frederick, 38
Chocolate Creams, 45–46, 47–48, 56, 57,
    59–60, 61, 62, 63, 65, 66–68, 72–75, 78,
    80, 81, 96, 101, 102, 114, 119
    see also, Christiana Edmunds, John
        Maynard
Church Street, 63, 78
Clapham Retreat, 22
Cobbe, Frances Power, 8
    experiences of school, 8, 9–10
Cockburn, Sir Alexander, 100
Cole, Harriett, 63, 95–96
Cole, Thomas Henry, 117, 136–137
Commissioners in Lunacy, 13, 17, 19, 21,
    145
Conolly, Dr. John, 18–19, 135
    The Treatment of the Insane Without
        Mechanical Restraint, 19.
Convict Lunatic Asylum (Tasmania), 133
Coroner, 60, 61
    see also David Black

Coultrop, Benjamin, 49, 52, 54, 101
County Asylum Act, 12
    inefficiency of, 12
Crecy, Edward, 55
Cross, Richard Assheton, 139
Curtis, William, 85, 90

Daniel, George Wythe, 15
Day, Mary Ann, 60–61, 63
Diggins, Henry, 49, 52
District Visitor, 56
Droit House, 2
Droitwich Lunatic Asylum, 16
Duke Street, 78

Edmunds (née Burn), Ann Christiana, 36,
    70, 71, 76, 82, 88–89, 90
    birth, 3
    marriage, 3
    children, 3–4, 36
    death of Frederick and Ellen, 4
    fails to sell house, 5, 16
    domestic responsibilities, 5–6
    role in education, 6
    has William removed to asylum, 12,15
    removes William to Peckham House, 15
    moves to Canterbury, 24
    syphilis, 35, 36
    Arthur Edmunds, 37
    moves to Brighton, 40
    concerns about Christiana, 28, 42–44, 82,
        83
    relationship with Dr. Beard, 48
    testimony in court, 116
    visits Christiana, 135, 137
    death, 145
Edmunds, Arthur Burn, 36, 37
    birth, 4
    diagnosed as epileptic, 33
    admitted to Royal Earlswood, 37
    death, 39, 41–42, 116, 126
Edmunds, Christiana, 44
    birth, 3
    at Mount Albion House, 6, 7–10
    returns home, 10–11
    threat of hereditary insanity, 22,
    coming out, 23
    hysteria, 28, 30, 31, 33, 103, 127
    paralysis, 30
    moves to Brighton, 40, 127
    neuralgia, 41, 53
    relationship with Dr. Beard, 42–44, 46,
        48, 68–71, 76, 101–102, 127

letters to Dr. Beard, 42, 47, 68–71, 76, 98, 101–102
plot against John Maynard, 48, 50, 52, 57, 64, 68, 71
poisons Emily Beard, 44–45, 47–48, 50, 51, 52, 57, 68–69, 83–84
poisons Benjamin Coultrop & Henry Diggins, 49, 52
poisons William Halliwell, 49–50, 52
purchases strychnine, 53–54, 57–58, 76–78, 96
see also, Strychnine, Isaac Garrett, Chocolate Creams
poisons Emily Baker, 55–56
complains to John Maynard, 56–57
poisons a dog, 58
poisons Sidney Barker, 59–60
poisons Harriett Cole, 63
poisons Caroline Walker, 63–4, 96
at Sidney Barker's inquest, 65–68, 69–70, 96, 119
as 'Dorothea', 71, 145
letters to Albert Barker, 72–76, 101
impersonates Glaisyer & Kemp, 76–78, 80, 96, 98–99
impersonates David Black, 78–79, 99
purchases arsenic, 79–80
see also, Arsenic, Isaac Garrett
interview with Inspector Gibbs, 80–81, 88–89
goes to Margate, 82–84, 96
poisons Boys family, 85, 86–87
other poisoned parcels, 85–86
arrest, 90, 114
at Lewes Prison, 91, 92,94, 96, 103–104, 105, 107, 117
see also, Lewes Prison
hearing 90–103
physical appearance, 92, 96, 101, 102, 104, 113–114, 120, 129, 131, 136
popular feeling against, 105, 123
possible motives, 55, 90, 94, 101, 109, 110, 116, 125,
insanity, 103–104, 109–110, 110–111, 117–118, 119, 123, 125, 126–127, 131, 140
at Newgate, 107–108, 112, 117, 122, 124, 129
trial, 103, 105, 112–122
breaks down, 116
found guilty, 120

treatment by the press, 192–93, 95, 108, 113, 123, 127–128, 141–142
pleads pregnancy, 120–122, 123
returns to Newgate, 122
petitions for mercy, 124–125
interviewed by Gull & Orange, 126–127, 129
sentence respited, 127, 128, 131
meets Sydney Cornish Harrington, 129–130
at Broadmoor, 131, 133–141
see also, Broadmoor Criminal Lunatic Asylum
smuggles contraband, 136–137
as vain and deceptive, 48, 71, 80, 82, 91, 136, 137–138, 140, 141
petitions her release, 139
ill-health, 140–141
Venus of Broadmoor, 141, 145
death, 141
historical reputation, 141–142
Narcissistic Personality Disorder, 143–144
Edmunds, Ellen, 36
death, 4
Edmunds, Frederick, 36
death, 4
Edmunds (née Harrington), Georgiana, (Christiana's sister-in-law), 26, 129, 130
Edmunds, Dr. James, 102–103
Edmunds, Thomas, 1
career of, 1
death, 2
Edmunds, William, 130
birth, 1
career, 2,3,
marriage, 2–3
children, 3–4
death of Frederick and Ellen, 4
decline in earnings, 4
fails to sell house, 5, 16
stops working, 5
becomes unwell, 11
assaults family doctor, 12
removed to Southall Park, 15
see also, Southall Park
returns home, 16
removed to Peckham House, 16
see also, Peckham House
treatment of, 20–1
General Paralysis of the Insane, vii, xii, 20

see also, General Paralysis of the Insane
syphilis, 34, 35, 36
see also, Syphilis
death, vii, 21, 30, 41–42, 116, 126
will, 23–24, 26
Edmunds, William (brother of Christiana
Edmunds), 36
birth, 3
at King's School, 6–7
medical career, 25
emigrates to South Africa, 25, 129
marriage, 25–26, 130
career, 135
death, 135
see also, Georgiana Edmunds
Ellis, Mildred, 14
Matron of Southall Park, 14
Ellis, Sir William C., 14
'Great Principle of Therapeutic
Employment', 14
Religious devotion, 14
Knighthood, 14
Death, 14
see also, Southall Park
Epilepsy, 29, 33, 39, 116
caused by masturbation, 33–34
Esmarch, Dr. Johann, ix, 34
Eyre, Jane, 39

'Fanny and Stella', 109
Female Sexuality, 29–30, 115
role in causing hysteria, 32
genital massage, 32
invention of vibrator, 35
see also, Women, Christiana Edmunds
Fisher, Marianna, 7
Food Adulteration, 46–48, 67
Bradford poisoning case, 47
Devon poisoning case, 47
Bristol poisoning case, 47
Foreman, Benjamin Edward, 38
marriage, 38
Foreman, (née Edmunds), Mary,
(Christiana's sister), 26, 36,
birth, 3
marriage, 38
children, 38
in court, 92, 95
correspondence with Christiana, 135–136
death, 145
Fournier, Dr. Jean Alfred, 33

Friend, Adelaide Ann, 83–84, 96
Galvanism, 31–33
see also, Hysteria
Garrett, Isaac, 41, 57, 78–80, 81, 94, 97, 114,
124
sells poison to Christiana, 53–54, 57–58,
76–78
goes to the police, 79
poisoning of, 85, 91
defends reputation, 103
General Paralysis of the Insane, vii, 20, 34,
35, 116
first clinical description, vii
symptoms, viii
causes, 34
role in asylum admissions, viii–ix
life expectancy of victims, viii
Gibbs, Inspector William, 60–61, 62, 65, 70,
79–81, 87, 94–95
early career, 60–61
interview with Christiana, 80–81 88–89
arrests Christiana, 91,
Gibson, John Rowland, 110
Glaisyer, Thomas & Kemp, John, 77–78, 79,
94
Gloucester Place, 42, 54, 56, 58, 71, 76, 78,
82, 85, 91
Governess, 26
society's attitude towards, 26
number of, 26
teaching subjects, 26–27
social status, 27
typical earnings, 27
Governesses' Benevolent Institution,
27–28
Grand Parade, 41, 46, 48, 64, 84, 85, 86–87
Graphology, 81, 97–100
see also, Frederick Netherclift
Gull, Sir William, 126–127, 129, 131
Guy, William, 101

Halliwell, William, 49–50, 52, 63
Hanwell County Asylum, 14, 19
Harrington, Sydney Cornish, 129–130
Haslam, Dr. John, vii
Hawley Square, 1, 3, 24, 25, 83
Helsey, Emily, 86
Hill, Dr. James, vii, 17–18
treatment of insane, 19–21
Holloway Sanatorium, 145
Holy Trinity Church, 2

Humphrey, Frederick, 87–88
Hunt, Mary Ann, 120, 121
Hysteria, 28, 44, 103
    definition of, 28
    'wandering womb', 28–29
    causes of, 32
    treatment, 30–33
    see also Female Sexuality, Galvinism

Inquest, 64
    Sidney Barker, 64–71, 80, 101, 102
    see also, David Black
Insanity,
    in general population, ix
    treatment of insane, 12, 15, 20
    county asylum movement, 12–13
    lunacy order, 15
    reform movement, 17–20
    use of cold bath, 20
    use of mechanical restraint, 18–19
    social stigma, 21–23, 103
    causes of, 21
    hereditary insanity, 22–3, 43, 48, 112,
        118–119
    criminal insanity, 109, 110–111, 128, 132–133
    'moral insanity', 111–112, 118, 134
    see also, Christiana Edmunds, William
        Edmunds

Jonas, Edmund, 107, 108, 110
Jones, Margaret, 134
Jones, Reverend Lloyd, 107

Kassovitz, Dr. Max, 36
    law on congenital syphilis, 36
    see also, Syphilis
Kebbell, Dr. William, 55
Kensall Green Cemetery, 21
Kent and Canterbury Hospital, 3
King's Road, 57
King's School, 6
Knatchbull, Sir Edward, 2
Knight, Margaret, 86–87, 94

Lamb, Charles, 94, 95, 96, 97, 99, 101, 124
Langdon-Down, Dr. John, 37–38
    see also, Royal Earlswood Asylum for
        Idiots
Laycock Dr. Thomas, 32
    see also, Hysteria, Galvinism
Lead, 47

Letheby, Dr. Henry, 62–63, 64, 65, 70
Levey's Bazaar, 2
Lewes Bonfire Society, 105
Lewes Prison, 91, 92, 94, 96, 103–104, 105,
    107, 126
    see also, Christiana Edmunds
Lime, Sulphate of, 47
Lithography, 97
    see also, Frederick Netherclift

Maden, Professor Tony, 143
Manning, Marie, 109
Marasmus, 39–40
Margate, 1, 24, 39, 40
    pier, 1–2
Margate Pier and Harbour Company, 3, 4
    scandal, 3
Margate Paving and Lighting Commission, 4
Marlborough Place, 41
Marsh, Dr. James, 50
Maudsley, Dr. Henry, 110, 118
Martin, Judge Baron, 105, 115, 119, 125
May, Adam, 78, 79, 95, 101, 119
Maynard, John, 47, 64, 66, 67, 68, 69, 70,
    72–75, 80, 114
    confectioner's shop, 45, 47, 49, 53, 56–57,
        59, 60, 61, 66–68, 75, 80–81, 101
    framed by Christiana, 48, 50, 53, 64, 68,
        71, 72–76
    see also, Chocolate Creams, Christiana
        Edmunds
McNaughtan, Daniel, 109–110
McNaughtan Rules, 109, 118
    see also, criminal insanity
Meadows, Annie, 59, 62, 67
Menopause, 44,
Menstruation, 21, 29, 31, 39
    role in causing hysteria, 29
Merrifield, John, 95
Metropolitan Police, 76
Meyer, Dr. John, 133
Miller, Charles, 59–60, 62, 65, 101
Miller, Ernest, 59–60, 62
Mills, Amelia, 86–87
Moon, William, 95
Moral Treatment, 17–20, 133, 135, 138
    vs. mechanical restraint, 18–19
    see also, Insanity
Moll Flanders, 106
Mount Albion House, 7–10, 30
    location of, 7

staff, 7
typical cost, 8
see also, Christiana Edmunds
Myrrh, 83

Narcissistic Personality Disorder
symptoms, 143–144
see also, Christiana Edmunds
Nash, James, 25
Netherclift, Frederick, 89, 97–100
see also, Graphology
Netherclift, Joseph, 97
Newgate Prison, 105, 106–108, 112, 121,
122, 129
history of, 106
description of, 106–107
Nicolson, Dr. David, 140
Noguchi, Dr. Hideyo, 34
North Road, 50
North Street, 56, 77, 80, 85

O'Connor, Patrick, 109
Old Steine, 86
Oliver, Fanny, 51
Opium, 52
Orange, Dr. William, 139
early career, 127
interviews Christiana, 126–127, 129, 134
at Broadmoor, 133, 134–135, 137, 138
retirement, 140
see also, Broadmoor Criminal Lunatic
Asylum
Over, Alice, 41, 42, 117
Over, George, 41, 42, 117

Page, Kate, 67
Palmer, William, 105, 112
Parry, John Humffreys, 110, 111–112, 114
career, 108–109
perplexed by Christiana, 115–116
Pavilion (Brighton), 80–81
Peckham House Lunatic Asylum, vii, 1, 23,
116, 130, 135
advertising, 16–17
condition of, 17
diet of patients, 21
Penfold, John, 66, 69, 70
Pettit, Charlotte, 58, 82–83, 84, 96
Pharmacy Act, 53, 79
see also, Poisoning
Physiognomy, 113–114

Pierce, William, 109
Pierlo, Eva, 107–108, 122
'Plead the Belly', 120
panel of matrons, 121–122
Poisoning,
public fascination, 93, 102, 112, 113
number of cases, 93
legislation, 52, 53, 79, 93
see also, Arsenic, Strychnine, Christiana
Edmunds
Poison Book, 53, 54, 78–80, 99
see also, Christiana Edmunds, Isaac
Garrett
Post-Mortem, 61
see also, Sidney Barker
Pownall, Thomas, 100
Prettyman, Mr, 30–31
Prichard, Dr. James Cowles,
on General Paralysis of the Insane, viii
on hereditary insanity, 22
on hysteria, 29
Private madhouses, 13
conditions in early madhouses, 13
for upper classes, 14
see also, Insanity
Prussic Acid, 52, 61

Queen's Road, 78, 95
Queen Victoria, 124

Railway, 40
Ramsgate Library, 7
Reinsch, Dr. Hugo, 51
Retreat, 18–20
Robben Island, 135
Robertson, Dr. Charles Lockhart, 110–111,
117–118, 119
Rodgers, Julian, 95, 100–101
Roupell. William, 97–98, 99
Rowland, Dr. Richard, 52
Royal Earlswood Asylum for Idiots, 37, 116
history, 37
treatment of patients, 37
Royal Pavilion, 40
Rugg, Richard, 60, 61–62, 65
Russell, Dr. Richard, 40
see also Sea-Bathing
Ryley, Dr. James Beresford, 121–122

Sale of Arsenic Act, 52
see also, Arsenic, Poisoning

Schweitzer, Julius, 57, 64, 80, 103
Sea-Bathing, 1, 40
Servants,
 in Edmunds' household, 5
 typical earnings, 5
 tasks, 5–6
Skey, Frederick Carpenter, 29
Smith, Walter, 87
Somerville, Mary, 9
 experiences at school, 9–10
Southall Park, 14, 116
 advertising, 14
 founding of, 14
 William Edmunds arrives 15
 typical cost, 16
 see also, Sir. William C. Ellis
Spring Gardens, 49, 54–56
St Andrews Asylum, 144–145
Stevens, Eliza, 39
Steward, Dr John Burdett, 15, 16
Stone, Caroline, 54, 57–58, 99, 114
Strychnine, 51, 52, 53, 54, 57–58, 62, 66, 67, 79, 100
 symptoms of strychnine poisoning, 45, 49, 50, 58, 63, 65, 77–78
 fatal dose, 51, 52, 57–58,
 uses, 51–52, 58, 65
 in criminal poisoning, 52
 similar to tetanus, 53
 sale of, 53–54, 57–58
 detection of, 62–63
 see also, Christiana Edmunds, Poisoning
Stuckey, William, 94, 95, 96, 97, 98, 101, 102
Surrey County Asylum, 133
Sussex Assizes, 103, 105
Sussex County Hospital, 41, 42, 86, 87
Syphilis, 34
 cause of General Paralysis of the Insane, ix
 symptoms, 34
 treatment, 34
 in marriage, 34–35
 procreation, 35, 36
 role in miscarriage, 36
 congenital syphilis, 35–36
 see also, William Edmunds

Tate, George, 29, 34
 Treatise on Hysteria, 29
Tatham, George, 85, 91
Taylor, Dr. Alfred Swaine, 125
Tilt, Dr. Edward, 44
Tissot, Dr. Samuel Auguste, 33
Tuke, James, 59–60
Tuke, William, 18–19
Turner, Richard, 131
Turpin, Dick, 106
Turrion, Caroline, 7
Tweedie, Dr. Alexander, 31
Tye, William, 56

Venetozza, Veronica, 7

Walker, Caroline, 63
Walker, Henry, 63
Warder, Dr. Alfred, 61, 63
Ware, George, 67, 68, 101
Watson, Reverend John Selby, 112
Wellesley, Arthur
Welsh, Nina, 26, 27
Wellington, Duke of, 3
 pavilion, 4
West Riding County Asylum, 14
West Street, 59, 60
White, George, 89–90, 91, 94
 makes public appeal, 89
White Hart, 1, 2
Willers, Dr. Jessen, ix, 34
Willis, Dr. Thomas, vii
Wolf's Bane, 61
Wood, Dr. William, 110, 124–125
Women,
 domestic ideals, 5–6, 7, 9–10, 93, 124
 as poisoners, 93
 executions of, 123–124
 in Broadmoor, 134
 see also, Female Sexuality

Zinc, 67, 70